INTROVERTS

The Magnificent Mind's Resource for Emotional,
Social, Professional, and Intellectual Success

(Successful Introverts, Conquer Fear, Extrovert
Society, Introverts Advantage)

Kristine Willbanks

Published by Harry Barnes

Kristine Willbanks

All Rights Reserved

Introverts: The Magnificent Mind's Resource for Emotional, Social, Professional, and Intellectual Success (Successful Introverts, Conquer Fear, Extrovert Society, Introverts Advantage)

ISBN 978-1-7751430-9-3

Legal & Disclaimer

The information contained in this book is not designed to replace or take the place of any form of medicine or professional medical advice. The information in this book has been provided for educational and entertainment purposes only.

The information contained in this book has been compiled from sources deemed reliable, and it is accurate to the best of the Author's knowledge; however, the Author cannot guarantee its accuracy and validity and cannot be held liable for any errors or omissions. Changes are periodically made to this book. You must consult your doctor or get professional medical advice before using any of the suggested remedies, techniques, or information in this book.

Upon using the information contained in this book, you agree to hold harmless the Author from and against any damages, costs, and expenses, including any legal fees potentially resulting from the application of any of the information provided by this guide. This disclaimer applies to any damages or injury caused by the use and application, whether directly or indirectly, of any advice or information presented, whether for breach of contract, tort, negligence, personal injury, criminal intent, or under any other cause of action.

You agree to accept all risks of using the information presented inside this book. You need to consult a professional medical practitioner in order to ensure you are both able and healthy enough to participate in this program.

Table of Contents

INTRODUCTION 1

CHAPTER 1: DISCOVER YOUR PERSONALITY 3

CHAPTER 2: WHAT IS IN AN INTROVERT'S MIND?? 10

CHAPTER 3: 10 COMMON MYTHS ABOUT INTROVERTS—
WHAT IT REALLY MEANS TO BE INTROVERTED 36

CHAPTER 4: EXTROVERT 101 44

CHAPTER 5: UNDERSTANDING INTROVERT ANXIETY 50

CHAPTER 6: WHEN YOU IDENTIFY AS AN INTROVERT...... 55

CHAPTER 7: INTROVERTS AT WORK 58

CHAPTER 8: A BLESSING IN DISGUISE? 72

CHAPTER 9: LEARN TO DISTINGUISH BETWEEN BEING
INTROVERTED AND BEING SHY 79

CHAPTER 10: WHAT ARE YOUR STRENGTHS AS AN
INTROVERT? 82

CHAPTER 11: THE STIGMA OF BEING AN INTROVERT 87

CHAPTER 12: THE CHALLENGES AND BENEFITS OF BEING
AN INTROVERT 89

CHAPTER 13: HOBBIES OF INTROVERTS............................ 99

CHAPTER 14: GOALS FOR LONE WOLVES........................ 103

CHAPTER 15: FRIENDSHIPS AS AN INTROVERT 110

CHAPTER 16: HOW TO PLAY TO YOUR STRENGTHS AS AN
INTROVERT... 114

CHAPTER 17: MYTHS ABOUT INTROVERTS 124

CHAPTER 18: OVERCOME YOUR PERCEIVED SHYNESS... 131

CHAPTER 19: THE INTROVERT'S SUCCESS PLAN............. 142

CHAPTER 20: THE CHALLENGES/ADVANTAGES WE FACE AS
INTROVERTS IN ROMANTIC RELATIONSHIPS 147

CHAPTER 21: MAXIMIZING INTROVERSION................... 150

CHAPTER 22: MEETING STRANGERS 162

CHAPTER 23: YOU DO NOT OWE ANYBODY EXPLANATIONS
ABOUT YOUR PERSONAL LIFE.. 173

CONCLUSION... 180

Introduction

Introversion is a state of mind: it's going within to experience the world around you. I believe this is exactly what we need to do to thrive as individual human beings and as a society as a whole. Too much time is spent in the outer world of our reality studying for exams, working up the next business plan, getting in extra hours to please our bosses, etc. This has lead to a decreasing number of people able to retrieve their personal power from within.

In this book not only will we completely eliminate once and for all the limitations associated with the worth 'introvert'. We will also grow to accept ourselves as introverts. I believe many have grown up renouncing their preference of introversion and wishing they were different. I was one of those cases. However, through experience, I have come to understand that the same thing I was ashamed of being had actually been my greatest strength all along. In this process of acceptance, we will take back our personal power and revise the potential for learning, relationship building, leadership, and spiritual growth that comes along with introversion.

Chapter 1: Discover Your Personality

It's time to stop and wonder... Why do some people like putting on make-up, or working out at the gym, or going to parties, while others like sitting on the couch and reading a book? Why do some people love to share embarrassing moments, while others... really get embarrassed about it? Why is it that some people can't say no to a challenge, love extreme sports, and will follow someone out into the parking lot to continue a debate, while others couldn't care less?

On a different note... Is self-improvement possible? If someone is bothered by their weaknesses, is there any GOOD plan out there to help? Why is it so hard to change? What is it people need to change? Understanding a little about personality answers all of these questions. Discovering your personality is the key to real self-improvement. It lets you understand better why you are the way you are... why you think the way you think and act the way you act. This empowers you to change, to improve yourself.

Once you know they way you work, you also discover how to make yourself work the way you want to work. Take cooking as an example. If you want to change a recipe, you need to first know the ingredients. People are the same way. If you want to change yourself, you first need to know the elements that affect how you act. Then, you can decide what is good, and what you want to add or take out to become better. Learning about personality can also help you understand how others think, and why some of them think differently from you. In addition to helping with self-knowledge and improvement, understanding personality, will also improve your relationships with others.

What is PERSONALITY?

There are numerous meanings to the word personality, but the one that applies to personality as used in this e Book, is: "the complex or characteristics that distinguishes an individual or nation or group, especially the totality of an individual's behavioral and emotional characteristics; a set of distinctive traits and characteristics".

Elements of Personality

There are four main personality types, or groups: choleric, sanguine, melancholic, and phlegmatic. Everyone falls into one of these main groups, or a combination of two of them. Remember: each persona is individual and unique, with special strengths and weaknesses. No personality type is better than any other. Within each personality type, there are many variations, and no two people, even people with the same personality type, are the same. There are as many personality variations as there are people. The personality groups are a guide, a way to know and understand yourself and others better.

Three main elements define the personality types:

Introverted/Extroverted

An introverted person lives within their own minds. They think they reflect and ponder. They tend to be more private people, more quiet people. They like the comfort of their home, and close group of friends. They like having alone time once in a while, so they have time to just think and sort through their thought and emotions.

An extroverted person, on the other hand, lives to be with people. They love to go out, to talk, to be at parties, to hear what other people have to say. While an introverted person thinks things through, and extroverted person talks them through. If an extroverted person is asked a question, that they've never thought of before, they may say, "I don't know," and then proceed to talk aloud nonstop until they reach their conclusion, or are distracted about something else. The extroverted person finds their fulfillment in being with people, and have a hard time being alone. Even when working on their own, they would rather work in a room with other people than by themselves.

People centered/principle centered

This element refers to what influences each person in making large decisions.

Some people are principle centered. They have different ideas, values, and principles that govern all of their decisions. If something is coherent with their principles, it is worth doing and supporting. If it conflicts with their principles, it is something to be fought against, or simply not supported. People who are principle centered will act based on their principles regardless of what other people think, and sometimes, regardless of how other people are affected.

People centered people are the opposite. They base the decisions and actions very much based on what other people think.

For them, the first value is pleasing the person. People centered personalities often don't have their principles thought out or expressed as thoroughly as principle centered personalities. Even when their principles are called into question, people persons are more likely to bend principle in order to please people. Principle centered personalities bend people to please principle. As we will see later, when discussing the different character types, both forms of influence have positive and negative points.

Primary/Secondary

A primary person acts first and thinks later - sometimes to their dismay. The primary person is quick to reach conclusions, quick to act, quick to feel, and quick to forget and move on. Their emotional resonance is sharp and intense, but frequently short lived. The primary person can go from laughing to crying to angry, and back to laughing again in a short period of time.

A secondary person thinks firsts, and acts later. They take longer to reflect, decide, act, and respond... but their response, particularly their mental and emotional response is of a longer, steadier duration.

Personality Types:

The four personality types combine these elements in the following way:

Choleric: extroverted, principle centered, primary

Sanguine: extroverted, people centered, primary

Melancholic: introverted, people centered, secondary

Phlegmatic: introverted, principle centered, secondary

Chapter 2: What Is In An Introvert's Mind??

"Introverts dislike small talk, but we are fluent in the language of ideas and dreams." ~ Michaela Chung

Introverts are like a special edition book, they

are not available for everyone, introverts like to share special occasions with just one person or only a few close friends, rather than having big celebrations. Introverts think that it would not at all be satisfying if they could have very close friendships with many people. They choose friends very thoughtfully and they are very picky in this task. Introverts prefer a few quality friends than making quantitively more friends.

Introverts try to structure their day so that they always have some time for themselves. I personally would not like to go for vacation in places where there are a lot of people around and where there are a lot of activities going on. After spending a few hours surrounded by a lot of people, I am usually eager to get away by myself that is not because I don't like people; it's just that I prefer myself not staying with them for too long. It is like people empty me; I have to get away to refill my soul. I rather be trekking on a lone mountain or visiting a secluded island to spend some time with myself or with someone who I feel comfortable with. Introverts think a lot, but theydon't say much. We should not underestimate an introvert because they are quiet; they usually know more than they say, they think a lot more than they speak and observe more than others supposedly know.

Many introverts love knowledge for its own sake, not necessarily as they may need it in future. In their lifetime they will learn stuff that they know that will never be used but still they will grab that piece of knowledge out of greed. People who think that introverts can't succeed in life because they lack social skills must understand that introverts have other desirable qualities like planning, innovation, creative writing and designing. This shows that everyone can shine, provided the right lighting, the way rice crops grow only in specific weather conditions.Let's clear one thing up that introverts do not hate talking because they dislike people, rather they hate the barrier talking creates between people, the way it may lead to debating and a potential conflict of interest. Introverts believe that the highest form of love is to be the protector of another person's feelings and to respect others opinions.

When you are an introvert and you've been lonely for a while, and then you find someone who understands you, you become really attached to them.It's only then that an introvert will start feeling comfortable around a person. Introvert conversations are like taking turns in badminton, each player gets to take their turn and play before the other player comes in and takes their turn. And their turns will be as short as it takes to hit a shuttle; it is not incorrect to say that the introverts are word economists in a society where most of the people are addicted of spending too much of words. If you ask an introvert what they want, they will probably say, "I want to be alone, by myself or with someone else who wants to be alone too." If you like to do things in a slow and steady way, don't let others make you feel as if you have to race. If you enjoy depth, don't force yourself to seek breadth, stay true to your own nature, be what you are not what others want you to be. Silence is beautiful, and it is not awkward, at times silence itself is a language and is far more effective than verbal communications.

After an hour or two of being socially on, we introverts need to turn off and recharge; we need to understand that this isn't antisocial and it isn't a sign of depression; it is just introverts' way for refueling themselves. Introverts restore their souls when they are by themselves. They do not have a strong need to be around other people. It is just, being around others and finding out about them is not one of the most interesting things they can think of doing. Introverts usually prefer to do things alone. So, they prefer others to remove themselves from their personal space. Only an introvert knows, how much better is silence; a book on the table, and the coffee cup. And how much better is one cup of coffee on the table than half a dozen. How much better is to sit alone in a corner like the solitary sea-bird that seldom opens its wings. Introverts are like, let me sit here forever with bare things, this coffee mug, this book and my solitude, when I can let myself be myself.

Introverts are very picky with whom they spend time with and whom they give their energy to, they prefer to reserve their time, intensity and spirit exclusively for those who they feel reflect sincerity. As a child, my happiest times were when I was left alone in the house on a Saturday afternoon while my family used to shop outside in the market. I believe solitude is only frightening to people who have obsessive compulsion of companionship, similarly silence is only frightening to people who are compulsively speaking. For introverts like me, silenceis ambrosia, it's a spirit of divinity.

Other people tend to misunderstand me, forming a mistaken impression of what kind of person I am because I don't say much about myself. I feel drained after social situations, even when I enjoyed myself. I enjoy analyzing my own thoughts and ideas about myself. I have a rich, complex inner life that no one except me will understand. I frequently think about random stuff, like when I am reading an interesting story or novel or when I am watching a good movie, I imagine how I would feel if the events in the story were happening to me.

Introverts usually think about themselves and that doesn't make them selfish,it's just there is an imaginary world in their mind where they are the only person in charge of the activities and situations around. They generally pay attention to their inner feelings. They value their personal self-evaluation, that is, the private opinion they have for themselves. Introverts have such a strong opinion about things that in almost all of the discussions they are right and when they are not right, they will try to find a middle ground and try to prove themselves partially correct.

I sometimes step back (in my mind) in order to examine myself from a distance. I daydream and fantasize, with some regularity, about things that might happen to me. I am inclined to be introspective, not just to analyze myself but to improve and reflect the best possible image of myself to the outside world. When I enter a room full of people, I often become self-conscious and feel that the eyes of others are upon me, the e-mail seems far more convenient than a telephone call. In order to avoid these never-ending phone calls, I would throw my phone away if I could get away with it.

My thoughts are often focused on episodes of my life that I wish I'd stop thinking about. My nervous system sometimes feels so fatigued that I just have to get off by myself. Most of the introverts are not at all confident about their social skills, whenever they have to go in a symposium or a conference, they have to prepare themselves mentally just to be with people. I am a sportsperson, but defeat or disappointment usually shame or anger me, but I try not to show it; I play to win and that's what matters. In order to make sure I win every time I compete; I will work harder than anyone else, I will practice a lot more than my workout schedule, I give my hundred per cent. It does take me forever to overcome my shyness in new situations, I feel ecstatic even in unfamiliar social situations, even when I am in a group of friends, I often feel very alone and uneasy. I struggle with things that come easy to other individuals like handshaking, hugging, or maybe getting examined by a doctor. I am pretty sure most of the introverts can strongly relate to these situations and they have gone through all these socially awkward and inner energy demanding situations.

My secret thoughts, feelings, and actions can be described as weird and they would horrify some of my friends. I feel painfully self-conscious when I am around strangers. I like to be off and running as soon as I wake up in the morning.I'll try anything once, as long as it is not something involving something like social interaction. For relaxation I like to slow down and take things easy, I like to work a lot and wear myself out with exertion. I often overthink before I could say anything that comes into my head. I generally seek new and exciting experiences and sensations. I like to keep busy all the time, when I am engaged in conversation just the idea of extending the dialogue or a potential future meeting horrifies me and I often act on the spur of the moment in such circumstances. At times, I intentionally hurt people because I am concerned about my draining energy and I focus on how to end the conversation as soon as possible without realizing the fact the other person may be expecting something from me like a piece of advice or confirmation.This is not just my story it's the story of all the introverts out there.

Introverts like to stand out and be unique, however they try suppressing this characteristic quality in situations which may potentially lead to an awkward outcome involving an unwanted conversation. Extroverts on the other hand sometimes do "crazy" things just to be different and to gain public attention. If you want to know how to be a better introvert or how to socialize being an introvert; try some of the things which provides a chance for you to conserve or to charge your energy levels, for instance online shopping is a really good option to save introvert energy. I like spending time with things, like when I go for shopping, I try not to interact with people, I would rather read the sign boards and the price tags while shopping, it is programmed in my personality. I don't usually tell people that I love to read books when they ask because if I do so, they will ask me what kind of books and a thousand other questions.

Whenever I think about speaking publicly, I am overwhelmed. If I am told to give a speech on stage, I would try faking it like an extrovert a million times in my head first and then I will have to practice and tell myself a thousand times that I can do this, before I can get on the stage. In order to be better at social gatherings and interactions I would train and fight with my own brain every single moment, it is not as easy for us as it seems to extroverts. Do I want to stay like this forever what should I do to channelize and use my energy my ideas and thoughts? I have indeed missed a lot of opportunities in my life just because I could not speak up and start a conversation with someone whom I should have approached. I like what I am, I enjoy it, and it is funny how people think that the life they live superior than mine, I don't know why they don't understand it's just a matter of choice. Instead of actually trying to interact with individuals at my workplace I would prefer putting my headphones on and playing video games.

I would like to be a leader and I would like to listen to my subordinates before making a decision, it will include a lot of conversation with team members that is one of the reason the idea of leading a team haunts me; I have no issues being a manager and handling responsibilities of a team it's just the team meetings and interactions that scare me. Introvertsdon't have any disadvantages; we are minority in general population but a majority in the gifted people. Studies show that people with higher than average IQ are often introverts. Here is a list of some of the most successful introverts: Albert Einstein, Bill Gates, Issac Newton, Larry page, Mark Zukerberg, Abrahm Lincoln, Mahatma Gandhi, Hilary Clinton, Warren Buffet, JK Rowling.

We must understand that the state of being an introvert is neither a disability nor it is any kind of neurological disorder.It doesn't matter if you are an introvert or an extrovert just like being right-handed or left-handed doesn't make you more or less talented. You are fabulous the way you are. In fact, introverts are considered good observer, planner and they do introspection way better than someone who is not an introvert.

We need to understand that why are we always made to think about our being, like we are always forced to think about why are we the way we are, we should rather think about what role society has to play in making people introverts. Why are introverts treated like people with some kind of disability, introverts are people who enjoy their own company, who believe that it's better to be in their own company and talk to themselves rather talking to someone with a lot lesser intellect. While talking introverts fear if others will be able to understand their perspective or not and process their idea the same way they themselves do. Due to the prevailing social stigma about introverts not being as good as their extrovert counterparts, some introverts try being equal, faking extrovert life. They are doing this to break the myth that introverts can't be sociable and theydon't have any friends. But in reality, we do have a gift of decent number of friends and remember, we believe in quality over quantity. I will like to have a friend who truly understand me rather than someone whom I have to explain my actions and choices all the time.It's not that I don't like all people, I am just a little bit choosy, we enjoy ourselves more than we enjoy others' company. We are not in a favor of spending all of the time with people instead we try spending time with ourselves as well. People think often that we are sadder than others, but no, we are not we just feel happy alone with our inner self. People think that we are not acceptable and are afraid of society, mass media, but in reality, introverts are the life of the groups; the puns, and the innovative jokes they crack are just hilarious. I would like to tell that don't judge a book by its cover because it is not necessarily applicable to all. Introverts choose to be alone, as it is entertaining for them. We like solitude, we like murmuring the favorite music, thinking or doing our daily chores and planning the things and events well ahead of time. That is entertainment for us, believe it or not.

Instead of having too much human interactions introverts like to have animal companions, and they make friends with fictional characters too. There are perks like they listen to us and introverts may talk to them whenever they want not when their friends want. We have great imagination, amazing listening skills, strong sense of self, deep thinking skills, and we don't panic if lost. Introverts are alarmed when their phone rings, they let it go on a voicemail; they ignore calls deliberately and text back, "sorry! I missed your call." Our future plans are not being the head of a company, but we plan to be in woods or mountains and embrace a transcendental life. I love being in my room, away from people at work. We prefer letting go the meeting without having to speak anything in it. We prefer sending an email instead of calling a meeting, or a conference call. Introverts will carry a book or look at their phone, pretend texting to deter people from talking to them. We are often excited about dating versus not wanting to be in a relationship.

I believe extroverts are verbose, they are the people who like using or expressing in more words than needed. On the other side introverts are laconic, we are the people who prefer using very few words. Some of the activities which are just normal for others but for introverts these are fun, like taking a shower, gardening, cooking, watching Netflix on weekends. Moreover, activities like sky gazing, walking under the stars, wanting and looking into void and overthinking are a few enjoyable things for introverts. Overthinking about things and dialogues on how we could have avoided a certain situation and what would be the outcomes, doing permutations and combinations of scenarios. Whenever I had to face a camera and speak something I would feel as if someone is trying to pull out heart out of my body, I could not understand why it is necessary for us to be so much social and talkative in front of a camera.

I was not really good with sarcasm initially however when I tried really hard, I became the master in it. Furthermore, at times I can't tell if my friends are serious or just pulling my leg. I would try to mash up with people and would wait to reach home and get into my room and read my books in addition to spending time with myself. Something we hate is being in a group, to be outgoing, and to engage with people.

If I try stay away from my books and I don't spend time with myself I would feel guilty about it, books are my friends and they need me too. How could I leave them waiting? I feel that they are calling me out.

The relationship that I have been into started online because if I can't even talk to a girl how would I woo her. Introverts are loyal lovers, if you be with an introvert, they are going to keep you forever; because it's really hard for an introvert to trust someone and be comfortable with someone. It's like climbing a mountain for them to find someone who understands them, so you can't find an introvert cheating on in relationships. Introverts take care of their loved ones a lot, they may not express it often but when they do, they don't care about what the world will think.

I could have told you a hundred other stories which are similar when I got the message that being myself the way I am is not socially acceptable, it's not a right way to do. But I had a feeling that it's not right, introverts are people too just like others, we have to learn some of the other traits like being bold and assertive too. I remember the time when I entered into a sales job, I don't know how I survived those 4 months of the job and I didn't make a single dollar sale. I would do the paper work and the collections that my boss or team mates would have finalized. Sharing documents with clients and getting them signed, dimensioning the rooms and making designs, this was what I used to do, and I was really good at these.

Almost all introverts wish to sit in the darkness and enjoy their own time. My roommate was an extrovert; he would talk to me like a parrot. I had to go outside and pretend that I am talking to my virtual girlfriend. The reason I never had a personal trainer in my gym is I don't want someone talking to me and telling me what to do. I made friends with Siri and Google assistant; I would find being in machine company much more amusing than being in human company.

I moved out of the place where I was staying because others in my apartment were too talkative and would ask me questions. Whenever someone or my roommates' friends used to come, I would just lock myself in the room and pretend that I am sleeping. It's a loss of society, science and the people, if we try to change and impose socially accepted behavior upon introverts. I am talking about the bias and the stigma that is pretty deep in our society and moreover it is real. Try to understand what it is, introvert-ism is how you respond to external stimulus. Extroverts crave stimulation whereas introverts feel that they are most alive when they are quieter and in more local environment.

These things are not absolute but most of the time it is correct. Our schools and offices are designed for extroverts leaving no space for introverts but to learn a few extrovert traits. No one in the interview asks if they are introvert or an extrovert, they may judge people just by their way of socializing but they may miss keeping in mind the things which are the plus points of being an introvert like creative mind and being well-planned team members who take lesser breaks for small talks. I believe all creativity comes from a mind and not from talking, introverts don't like talking about how someone is planning their weekend or how good/bad the weather is going to be; they would rather discuss about ghosts, aliens, atoms, galaxies, life, philosophy, something that can keep you awake at night. As a kid in school, we used to sit in rows, I would stare and try to be mean with my fellows so that people don't try to interact with me.

We try finding different solutions to stay away from conversation, we would rather channelize our energy in studies and sports. Study before a teacher teaches in the class in order to avoid conflict with the teacher in trying to clarify doubts. I started to ask teachers questions so that they won't ask anything from me. I would attend the classes so that I don't have to talk to my friends over the phone; I would prefer texting instead in case I had something to clarify. I would rather avoid being in a relationship because that requires a lot of talks. I preferred athletics over team games, however if I felt like playing soccer, I would rather play it in my lone time by practicing dribbling skills just to avoid interactions with more people.

Vast majority of teachers think subconsciously that the extroverts are better students and not introverts. However, on the flip side, introverts get better grades and are more knowledgeable according to research. In corporate world we have to communicate with members; work in groups instead of working alone. we work in open plan offices and not in private cubicles anymore. Where we are subject to noise and gaze of the coworkers, lectures on improving leadership and presentation skills. Introverts are proven to be really good leaders in some scenarios as they are very careful, not risk takers, they play safe and are stable leaders. There are better outcomes, when teams are manageable and leaders let the subordinates think, speak and decide accordingly. Extroverts are like bosses, and they get over excited about their own ideas.

Extroverts d on't usually enjoy electing or asking their subordinates because they were to deliver what they wanted to. There is zero correlation between being the person with the best ideas and being the best talker. Free the ideas from the fear of group distortion and then discuss the original ideas to brainstorm eventually come up with a conclusion, together as a team.

We, the introverts might not easily bubble up on the surface. Introverts are soft spoken yet they are powerful. Pure introvert or an extrovert personality doesn't exist, amalgamated ambiverts are the best that can exist in a society,that's what I believe. I have observed that excess of anything is bad, it holds true for personality traits as well, we should not be more of yin or more of yang; just try maintaining the balance will make you perfect. People believe that the solitude is ingredient of creativity because many ideas come when you are alone. Introverts are more reserved persona; and solitude matters for us and it's really important for us to feel alive. We have strangely forgotten to think about being alone and giving ourselves our personal time.

In major religions, you will find seekers. You can't focus and meditate in a group you have to be alone and focus all your energy on yourself to achieve that. We have known for centuries the transcendental power of solitude. Psychology says that is better to be alone and let your brain wander, we have to surrender our senses and worldly relations to get full control over our inner world. Go to wilderness, to reveal what we have. Contemporary, there are people who try doing group meditation; which I believe is an insane idea. You can't really focus on energy by being with people with different wavelengths and vibes, you need to be by yourself to truly reach the meditative state.

Chapter 3: 10 Common Myths About Introverts—What It Really Means To Be Introverted

The problem with some people is that they judge introverts too much without really knowing what it means and how it feels to be introverted. In this chapter, you'll learn about 10 common myths about introverts and what the truths about them are.

Myth #1: Introverts are shy!

Truth: Probably the biggest misconception about introverts is that they are shy people. This is wrong! Some celebrities such as Audrey Hepburn, Johnny Carson, Johnny Depp and Will Ferrell have all admitted to be introverts—and yet, they were able to carve their own niches in the entertainment industry. Being an introvert doesn't mean that you're afraid of people—you just choose the people whom you'd like in your life. People think that introverts are shy because they don't like to start conversations but if you talk to them, they will actually respond to you and they can keep the conversation going, too.

Myth #2: Introverts will never be good leaders

Truth: Even if research has it that around 80 percent of leaders are those who are extroverts, it does not necessarily mean that introverts are meant to be followers their whole lives and that they can never be great leaders. Introverts and extroverts are equally good as leaders—it all depends on their leadership style and how they choose to manage their people or their companies. Introverts can be effective leaders because they concentrate on what they have to do and they think clearly. General Charles Krulak, who used to be Commandant of the US Marine Corps, is an introvert, and so is Doug Conant, Campbell Soup's former CEO.

Myth #3: Introverts dislike all kinds of people

Truth: Introverts do not dislike everybody. They just know how to quantify people and aren't worried about not being "friends" with everyone because they know that few close friends are always better than having just "acquaintances". Introverts value the people they have in their life and are very much loyal and faithful—those are the reasons why they make such good friends and partners in relationships. Introverts like people with substance and people who know the value of respect.

Myth #4: Introverts are rude

Truth: Just because introverts don't talk right away or because they do not choose to be "friends" with everybody does not mean that they are rude. They just like to process their thoughts first and make sure that they are able to say the right things instead of talking without thinking and getting to hurt the people around them. They don't like to talk just for the sake of talking. When they talk, they will get your attention and you will have to listen to them because what they say contains a lot of essence. This is the reason why they are often thought of as aloof or not interested when in fact; they're just summing their thoughts up and are just smart, significant individuals.

Myth #5: Introverts like to be alone all the time

Truth: Introverts like to be alone, yes, but of course, they also enjoy the company of others from time to time. Introverts are day-dreamers. They enjoy reflecting on the state of their lives and even like working on tests or puzzles. Does this mean that they're boring individuals? Of course not. As they say, no man is an island. When introverts find people who share their same ideals, passions and even like the same things that they like, of course, they will talk to them. They're normal people, too—even if they crave solitude more than others do.

Myth #6: Introverts hate going out in public

Truth: Research has it that there are some introverts who love going out and who find it therapeutic to go to their favorite bookstores, parks and other public places. Maybe introverts don't like spending so much time in public but it's only because they know that there are better things to do with their time rather than spend it gossiping about who knows what. They are the kinds of people who shut down when there is too much going on so they need to recharge after being in a public place. Once introverts have recharged by going home, spending some time alone and doing what they have to do, they're ready to go out again. Plus, there are pretty much 40 to 50 percent of students who are introverts. If they can't stand public places then surely, all of them will probably be homeschooled instead of attending regular school.

Myth #7: Introverts are weird

Truth: Do you enjoy movies? Introverts do, too. Are you bopping your head to the latest hit on the radio? Introverts are doing the same thing, too. Have you been reading what's new about your favorite stars? Introverts read up on them, too. Introverts aren't weird—they are just non-conformists. They don't like "following the crowd". They know how to stand on their own, believe in what they believe in and they know that it's important to remain true to oneself instead of getting lost in the crowd. They don't follow what's "trendy" just for the heck of it; they make their own decisions.

Myth #8: Introverts don't know how to have fun and have a hard time relaxing

Truth: You know what's great about introverts? They don't need lots of people to be happy; they can be happy even if they're just at home, watching the television or even if they're just reading their favorite books. They're not naturally thrill seekers but they know how to be happy and how to enjoy what they have.

Myth #9: Introverts cannot be in relationships

Truth: Of course, they could. Introverts can meet people, hang out with them, start dating them and get together with them. Introverts can get married and have happy and healthy relationships. They are capable of being good parents and great partners for life.

Myth #10: Being an introvert is a mistake; it's like a disease that can be fixed

Truth: Why would you fix something that isn't even broken? Again, there's nothing wrong with being an introvert. It isn't a mistake and it's not something that you have to fix. Some artists, musicians, poets, doctors, filmmakers, philosophers, writers and politicians are introverts—what do you think the world would be like without them? You don't need to fix introverts— they are already great by just being themselves. They deserve respect for being who they are—just like everyone else deserves respect for being who they are, too.

Chapter 4: Extrovert 101

In the previous chapter, you learned about your introversion; like what it is, and what it is not. Now, you will be learning about the kind of person whom you think you want to become more like, the extroverts. Again, it is near impossible for an introvert to make a 180-degree turn and become a complete extrovert, but it is possible for them to acquire some of their traits. To understand further how you can become more extroverted, you must first learn what kind of people extroverts really are.

Some introverts think that extroverts are noisy, talkative, and downright annoying, but for others they are sociable, energetic, and a pleasure to be with. Although these observations have some tinge of truth to them, they are not what extroverts are all about; yes, just like you they are complex beings.

Extroverts are energised when they are around other people

Extroverts are obviously the polar opposites of introverts; they get their energy by being around other people, while introverts, like you, feel more alive when all alone. What most introverts mistakenly believe about extroverts is that they crave attention, and that they would do anything just to be in the limelight. However, that is not entirely true. Extroverts enjoy the attention, but they value the chance to socialise with other people more.

Unlike introverts, when an extrovert cannot stand being alone for extended periods. They get bored easily and become fidgety when they are all alone.

When looking for a solution to a problem they would rather discuss things with others rather than ponder on it alone

Extroverts have a different way of dealing with problems; they ask other people for suggestions. Unlike introverts who like to stew on their problems alone until a solution comes to them, extroverts like to talk with their friends so they can come up with the best answer to their dilemma. They gather different ideas from their peers, compare their answers, and then choose one answer (or a combination of ideas) that suits them best.

This makes extroverts great team players because they like sharing their ideas with others.

They are easy to get along with

Introverts will only share their innermost feelings to the people whom they are closest to, while extroverts would readily chat with anyone who is willing to listen. This does not mean that extroverts are loose-lipped; they still know how to keep secrets. What this means is that they can easily communicate with other people; they somehow know what they need to do to illicit a response from others.

Is there such a thing as "shy extroverts?"

This may come as a shock to most introverts, but yes, many extroverted people are also shy. Who are they?

They are the ones who like to chill in the background during parties. They like being around people, but they do not socialise that much. They are often wrongfully branded as weirdoes and creepers because they just stand there and watch people, but it does not necessarily mean they have creepy thoughts, that's just the way they are.

They are the ones that do not talk much, but delight in conversations. You can talk with them all night, and they will only nod and utter a couple of words the entire time, and yet you feel that he/she enjoyed spending time with you.

They like one-on-one conversations. Shy extroverts are the masters when it comes to coffee shop chats or late night phone calls. Shy extroverts will not have any second thoughts when you ask them out for coffee or shopping, in fact, they would be more than delighted if you do. These people are the ones who delight at the thought of coming back to their hometown so they can catch up with their old friends and relatives.

They are awkward at social gatherings. This may come as a shock for most introverts, but not all extroverts know how to handle themselves well during social events, some of them do not even have passable social skills to begin with. Yes, it is true that extroverts enjoy being in the company of others, but that does not make them masters when it comes to interacting with others, quite a number of them do not know how to carry themselves when in public. However, what makes them different from introverts is that they rarely care what they look like as long as they are enjoying themselves.

If you see these traits within you then you might not be an introvert at all, you just might be an extremely shy extrovert. If this is the case, you just need to work on your social skills. However, if you truly are an introvert, then this will take a bit more work.

All introverts have a small amount of extroversion within themselves, and this is why you are reading this book right now, because your inner extrovert wants to get out. The only problem is that your introverted side, which is your dominant character trait, is keeping your extroversion from showing.

The following chapter will focus on the obstacles that are preventing you from becoming a more extroverted kind of person. By focusing your attention to these hindrances, your efforts will become a bit more efficient and effective.

Chapter 5: Understanding Introvert Anxiety

Introverts have the reputation of being the odd man out in the group. In social settings, you will usually find them alone. The other people cannot or will not talk to them because they are unsure if the introvert even wants to talk. The introvert on the other hand, is afraid to start a conversation because they feel like they do not have the necessary communication skills to carry a conversation.

Because they lack confidence in their socialization skills, anxiety starts to creep in when introverts have to interact with the people around them. Anxiety is a common emotion. It only becomes a problem when it becomes chronic. Some introverts may have a chronic anxiety problem before starting interactions with other people.

How anxiety works

Just like most of our negative behaviors, anxiety activates our fight or flight response. The human brain triggers this response when it perceives a threat to its survival, regardless if it is real or not. It is called the fight or flight response because an organism in this state usually has two options, to run away from the threat or to face it and fight it.

Introverts are prone to the flight response when facing the possibility of social interactions. Instead of starting a conversation with their seatmate on a train or airplane, for example, introverts prefer to keep quiet.

Because they have been avoiding new social interactions for a while, introverts have developed a habit of running away from the uncomfortable situation of starting a conversation. If your life goals require that you interact with people regularly, you will need to work on changing this habit.

It is all in the mind

When we are about to interact with a stranger and our mind initiates the fight or flight response, we begin to feel uncomfortable. It is our mind's way of telling us that there is a possible threat in the environment.

However, the truth is that there is no threat whatsoever. In our modern society, social interactions rarely end up in life threatening scenarios. You can only benefit from the communication skills that will be enumerated in the succeeding chapters if you accept the following:

1. Social interactions are harmless

2.They are necessary for reaching your goals

3.Most importantly, start believing that you can overcome your anxiety

If you believe these three points, your fear of talking and interacting with others will be greatly alleviated. Even if you feel uncomfortable at first, you can overcome your anxiety and take steps to improve your social interactions.

You already know how to socialize

Most introverts have their own circle of friends. They have a group of people that they are comfortable communicating with. When interacting with this group, they can be their true selves. They do not hold back or allow anxiety to control their behavior.

You should examine your own circle of friends. You should look into your own behavior when interacting with people you are comfortable with. You already have social success when you are interacting with these people. Most of the time, introverts only need to simulate their confidence in this circle of friends with other social networks.

You should also examine how you feel when you are with the people you are comfortable with. When we are with these types of people, we usually let our guard down. We even show signs of being vulnerable like showing emotions.

As you widen your circle of friends, you will need to emulate this feeling with other people. There are times when you need to show vulnerability to gain the trust of certain groups. You should be ready for these kinds of scenarios.

Chapter 6: When You Identify As An Introvert...

People who identify themselves as introverts cope in various ways.

Some have fully accepted that they simply prefer a smaller circle of friends, since they are less demanding company. They take more time to themselves (to recharge), do work that suits their personality traits and build relationships based on what is comfortable.

Some work to develop extroverted traits to find a balance in the personality spectrum. They think this will help them fit into the modern world's expectations where extroverted traits are more rewarded. They push themselves to socialize more to develop the needed communication skills.

Some get psychiatric help for a possible disorder. They will initiate therapy in their lives or try prescriptions designed for mental   health.

Some will be settling for a while. They continue to have difficulty developing their ideal relationships and never find a way to solve their problems due to poor advice or overwhelming amount of information. Some are also too discouraged, anxious, hurt or traumatized to attempt new relationships and challenges.

And there will be some that undergo a life-changing experience, either something inspirational or painful. This provides them the profound motivation to make extreme changes in their lives.

What if you never learned about the concept of introversion? How would you cope?

You will soon realize that the value and belief systems that you implement into your lifestyle affect your self-concept profoundly. This influences the kinds of choices you make in regards to your self-development and relationships.

Keep these in mind when you read on.

powerful emotional life with your partner. Draw on that connection in order to calm your partner and get him/her to listen to your point of view as well.

Chapter 7: Introverts At Work

Simple strategies for getting noticed, speaking up and thriving at work

No matter what kind of work you do, being an introvert in the workplace has very real challenges. Most traditional workplaces are highly collaborative settings where you're expected to chime in, speak up, grab the spotlight and engage frequently with co-workers for large chunks of time. For introverts who thrive when working solo and need lots of time to recharge, the modern workplace can be a noisy, overwhelming place.

No matter what kind of work you do, there are small steps you can take to make work a more hospitable place. Let's go over some simple strategies that will help you find your sweet spot at work.

The Art of Getting Noticed

Here's a story that still makes me cringe. Back in my college days, I took an office temp job at a law firm to make money during the summer. I was the "copy girl," spending hours pushing the big green button on the copy machine, collating large files and trouble-shooting the massively outdated office copier every time there was a paper jam (which was often). After two months of copying, stapling and un-jamming, I was tasked with delivering a huge copy order to one of the partners, whom I had passed in the hallways dozens of times. I had shared a lunch table with this man more than once, but generally just ate my sandwich and listened to my co-workers talk. When I delivered the copy order to him, Mr. Law Firm Partner squinted up at me said, "Are you new here? What's your name?"

Now, I was a college temp whose sole work duty was to make copies all day – the quiet copy girl in the back room. I didn't expect to make a huge impression on anyone in that capacity, but it still smarts when you realize you haven't made any impression at all.

No one wants to be invisible at work. If you're having trouble leaving your mark or gaining the recognition you deserve, here are some simple strategies to help you get noticed:

- Set target goals every day – then crush them. Start with small goals. For example, set a goal that you will talk to two co-workers that you don't usually get a chance to talk with. This can be casual small talk ("How was your weekend?"), a compliment, a question – anything to get to know your co-workers better, and help them know you better. It only takes a couple of conversations to transition from being "Tim the quiet IT guy" to "Tim, my co-worker who has a Jack Russell Terrier named Terry and loves Indian food."

- Make your mark at the next meeting. Do you spend most company meetings doodling on your yellow legal pad? Meetings, especially large group meetings, can cause some introverts to fade into the background. Resist the urge to go silent. A group meeting is the easiest, most efficient way to make a very real impression on everyone in your organization. Come up with one or two relevant questions, suggestions or comments. Make it a point to speak up at least once.

- Share your gifts at work. Introverts tend to be deep listeners and sharp analysts. It may surprise you to learn that introverts also often make excellent salespeople — being a good listener makes it easier to hear what clients are saying and anticipate their needs. Pinpoint your strengths and make it a point to show them off at work. Look for ways to stretch your talents at work in way that go beyond your job description.

Even if your position doesn't necessarily involve speaking to clients or other people directly, find opportunities to use your creativity and analytical gifts. No matter what role you're currently in, chances are you can find ways to highlight your best attributes in ways you haven't done before. For example, if you love to write (many introverts do), aim to impress with your reports, sales letters, or emails that show off your sparkling prose. Put your name on reports.

- Practice bragging. Okay, maybe not bragging exactly. But definitely aim to become more comfortable with talking about your personal accomplishments and professional achievements. Make a list of everything you are truly proud about. Don't be afraid to share what you've learned and what you've done. Many introverts tend to be reserved about past accomplishments, fearful of coming off as boastful. But most people want to learn more about you – especially employers who may not realize the full scope of your talents and skills.

- Take the lead. Most introverts aren't naturally drawn to the spotlight, but that doesn't mean you don't have the makings of a strong leader. In fact, several studies show that introverts do well when leading groups of engaged workers. Introverts listen well and thus tend to implement good ideas when they hear them. Introverts are also good at building strong one-on-one relationships with team members. If you're feeling invisible at work, keep these assets in mind and offer to take the lead on the next project.

If the idea of leading a team or spearheading a project sounds intimidating, start small with a low-stakes leadership opportunity. Does your company do volunteer work? Why not take the lead on the next food drive, clothing drive or other charitable initiative? This will give you the opportunity to flex your leadership muscles in a low-pressure setting.

- Schedule a one-on-one. Most introverts communicate best in intimate settings. If your organization doesn't already schedule one-on-one meetings, take the initiative and ask for a meeting with management to discuss ideas, voice concerns or simply to ask how you're doing and check in.

Carve Out Your Own Personal Quiet Zone

Today's modern workspaces are geared toward extroverts. Remember Don Draper's private office – complete with bar cart, couch and locking door - in Mad Men? Ah, we can dream, right? Most introverts work best when they have a quiet work space that allows them to work independently for long stretches of time. Unfortunately, today's modern office is all about the open floor plan. Cubicle partitions have never been lower, and privacy is almost non-existent. How is an introvert supposed to thrive in a hectic, open floor plan where constant stimulation is the order of the day?

- Do your best to accommodate your needs, so that you can do your best work. If you're having trouble focusing, ask to work in a conference room or other quiet space. If it's acceptable in your workplace, bring headphones to work and use them to block out noise or play ambient music to help you focus. Ask for what you need. It might feel awkward at first, but many office managers don't realize that some workers will be most productive and creative in a quiet, more private space. Work within your workplace's boundaries to carve out a workable space.

- Take frequent, short breaks. Introverts are prone to burn out, so be mindful if you work in an especially hectic workplace. That means you need to take several pauses throughout the day to recharge. Go for a walk outside, if possible. Move between activity and rest at steady intervals. Time yourself if you need to.

- Make work alliances. That's not just a fancy way of saying you should make friends at work (although that's always a good idea). Your chances of thriving at work increase exponentially when you are able to make deep, meaningful connections at work. If you have a manager, be open about how you work best. Most researchers believe that roughly half the world population is on the introversion spectrum – that means the chances you are surrounded by at least one fellow introvert is quite high. Seek out colleagues that you feel comfortable talking to, and with whom you can discuss things other than work. Touch base with them regularly. The goal here is finding people that you can be "quiet" with.

- Avoid caffeine – at least before big meetings or looming deadlines. In his fascinating book Me, Myself, and Us: The Science of Personality and the Art of Well-Being, psychologist Brian Little cited research indicating that introverts who consume coffee during periods of high stimulation perform less optimally than their extrovert counterparts. The theory here is that introverts are already stimulated during stressful periods, so the extra caffeine kick causes us to fizzle out faster. Know your body and feed it for optimal performance, especially during periods of intense work.

- Prepare, prepare, prepare. Remember the story about my Skype job interview? I was able to perform well because I spent several hours researching my potential employer, reading about job interview strategies, and making a short list of talking points and accomplishments that I could discuss with (relative) ease during the interview.

If you know you have a big deadline, presentation, meeting or other high-pressure work project on the horizon, make it a habit to prepare. This might mean working ahead so that you don't end up cramming at the last minute. Or it could mean taking extra care to eat and sleep well during this period so that you know your body and mind can meet the demands.

Are You in the Right Place?

Are you feeling permanently burned out? Do you spend all Sunday night dreading having to go into work on Monday morning? If you find yourself persistently unhappy with your workplace and career, I want to gently suggest that you ask yourself the following question: Am I in the right place?

Years ago, I was working in the cramped offices of a fledging radio network as a staff writer. The pace was fast, furious and relentless. Management was elusive; our boss was always on assignment, on vacation, or else locked in her office on the other side of the building. I sat on a squeaky office chair, jammed around a conference table with eight other people. When my co-worker sneezed, I felt the rush of wind on my forearm. I dreamt longingly for a private office. Heck, a cubicle seemed like paradise. The fast pace, lack of communication, cramped musty office and lack of privacy weighed on me daily. Those weren't the main reasons I eventually resigned from that position to move to another company, but they certainly were factors.

If you find your work environment to be consistently inhospitable and difficult to work in, maybe it's time to find a better fit. I can tell you from personal experience that I was able to find a workplace that aligned much better with my values, attributes and needs, and you can too.

Introvert Career Paths

Introverts can and do thrive in all career paths. Take a look at this list of famous introverts, just to get a sense of the remarkable and varied work that introverts have accomplished:

- Audrey Hepburn
- George Stephanopoulos
- Albert Einstein
- Bill Gates
- J.K. Rowling
- Mahatma Gandhi
- Warren Buffet

That's a pretty impressive list, right? One common denominator we can glean from this short list is that many introverts are drawn to creativity and autonomy. If you're seeking a new career path, know that many introverts thrive in fields that emphasize close attention to details, independence and ample time alone. If you're just starting to blaze your own career path, or looking for a change, here are some careers where introverts tend to shine:

- writer/editor
- web developer
- artists (painters, sculptors, illustrators)
- private chef
- geologist
- animal care technician
- social media manager
- forester
- court reporter
- graphic designer
- electrician
- mechanic
- entrepreneur

Obviously, introverts have a place in all fields and industries. But hopefully, if you have ever felt like you don't belong at the office (or studio, or garage, or underwater vessel – or wherever it is that you do your work), be firm in knowing that there are endless possibilities and it's never too late to start over.

Chapter 8: A Blessing In Disguise?

While introversion gets a bad rap, there is a lot of merit to it. As an introvert, you have an advantage over other people. The problem is that most of us focus on the reasons it is wrong to be an introvert. We forget that to every coin, there are two sides.

Like said in Chapter 1, some of the world's most extraordinary breakthroughs have come from introverts. And even some of the greatest artists, leaders, dancers, etc., are introverts. The success of these people could not be mere accidents. But something to do with the way they think and interact with their world.

You Are Good at Nurturing Relationships

This may come as a surprise. But introverts make some of the world's best friends. Remember, it is not that introverts hate people. Rather, they do not like people who share nothing in common with them.

To an introvert, the quality of a friendship is more important than anything else. There is no value in having lots of friends if you don't have a connection with any of them.

In addition to this, the fact that introverts like to listen attentively enables them to make other people feel understood. This creates a strong bond that enhances the quality of the friendship. Furthermore, the attentiveness allows introverts to understand other people more deeply. They get to know what motivates them, how they think, things they don't like, etc.

Capable of Coming Up With Great Ideas

Being alone enables introverts to really think about things in their own way. Research has found that thinking in groups rarely creates any new ideas. That's because we tend to be influenced by what others are thinking. Furthermore, there is the fear of what others may think about your ideas. So to avoid being embarrassed, you restrict your thoughts to think like all those around you.

In solitude, however, you do not have the pressure of others. You are free to roam in any way. And if your ideas suck, there is no embarrassment in that.

Easier to Achieve Mastery

Another great trait among introverts is the ability to fully focus on a single task. They say it takes 10,000 hours to achieve mastery. While I don't believe this, I believe the more you focus on something, the higher the chances that you will get good at it in no time.

This focus allows introverts to be masters in the field they choose. It may be music, acting, writing, etc. Haven't you ever wondered why some of the greatest artists are introverts? Is it a coincidence? It may or it may not be.

Good Knowledge of Things

It is an introvert's nature to know things. The time they spend alone allows them to question things they would not bother about if hanging with other people. This creates curiosity. And that curiosity leads them on a quest for knowledge.

That is the reason introverts like to read books. They like to know how the universe operates. They like to understand how people think.

Thinking before Talking

As an introvert, you can come out as the wise one in the midst of fumblers. When others are freaking out, talking uncontrollably, you first take time to consider facts and work out possible solutions. This is a much-desired trait. It enables you to give the right advice to others when they need it. It helps you stay on the right path when trouble comes knocking.

And this has many practical uses. For example, it can help your relationships become stronger. In business, you can be sure to not indulge in risky activities that may doom your business into extinction.

Even as a leader, you can be confident to show others the right way.

You Are More Self-Aware

We all need to understand what drives us. We need to be aware of our feelings and emotions. And for introverts, the time they spend alone is enough to gain this understanding. Being by yourself lets you connect with your thoughts. You can ask yourself why you are feeling a certain way. Why you chose to do something instead of another.

This self-reflection also gives you the power to correct your errors. You become a better person since you reduce chances of committing the same mistakes.

Why You May Need To Come Out

While you must embrace your introversion, we also need to acknowledge that it is important to interact with others from time to time. You do not have to turn yourself into an island. Humans are social animals. If you spend too much time by yourself, you will soon start feeling lonely. And that is not healthy.

Social Connections Are Good for Health

Studies have proved time and again that having strong social connections is good for your health. You can lower your stress levels, boost your immunity, and slow the aging process. Other studies also show that those with strong social connections live long.

However, this does not mean you must know everyone in your neighborhood or go to every party happening around you. Quality trumps quantity when it comes to friends. So go after the right friends. These can be your relatives, your co-workers, or even strangers.

Good for Your Professional Life

While education is important for your career, it is no guarantee that you will find a job or advance in your profession. Sometimes, things come down to knowing someone who knows someone with the potential to promote you or give you a job opportunity.

You may consider this cheating or unfair, but it is the reality of how information spreads. Not all job opportunities are advertised in newspapers or job boards. So having strong social connections is important.

Advance Your Romantic Relationships

There comes a time when you will need a partner to hang by your side. However, if you lock yourself in your room, you will limit your chances of finding the perfect him or her. Sometimes, being in a good relationship is a numbers game. Going out allows you to have an option. You are likely to find the perfect partner.

Chapter 9: Learn To Distinguish Between Being Introverted And Being Shy

One of the biggest myths about introverts is that they don't like to talk to people or to interact socially. While this may be true of some introverts, it is certainly not true of all of them. In fact, there are many introverts who don't fall into the so-called textbook definition since they are outgoing and like social interaction – just not too much of it and not all the time. For instance, Barbra Streisand is known for her larger-than-life extrovert personality, but also has to battle with bouts of crippling shyness. Bill Gates, on the other hand, is an introvert but not shy since the opinions of others don't bother him.

Psychologists define shyness as a form of social anxiety in which sufferers are afraid of being negatively judged by others. Introversion, on the other hand, is a condition in which a person prefers environments that are quiet and have minimal stimulation. In fact, the Diagnostic and Statistical Manual 4th edition recognizes shyness as an illness provided the anxiety the sufferer feels has started to significantly interfere with the performance of their work or if they display "marked distress" about their condition.

Why is it important to make a distinction between shyness and introversion? Because shyness can be a crippling condition for which the sufferer may need to seek help, while introversion is not. The introvert does not avoid social interaction because they fear it, but simply because they prefer it. Understanding the difference not only helps you understand your introversion more deeply, it also helps you avoid misunderstanding. After all, there are people who would say, "But you like talking to people, how can you be introverted?" and thus treat you as if you were just being a killjoy when you say you don't want to go out or attend a party.

In short, being an introvert does not mean that you have to conform to the commonly accepted stereotype, which confuses introversion with shyness or treats them as if they were interchangeable. Just because you are not shy does not mean that you are not introverted as well. And being introverted does not mean that you will not experience occasional moments of social anxiety. You simply have to learn to respect who you are and learn how to use your natural temperament to live the best life that you can.

Chapter 10: What Are Your Strengths As An Introvert?

Ask most introverts and they'll tell you about a time when they were made to feel abnormal because of their innate need for solitude. This chapter discusses the strengths of introverts, and since introverts are thought to be quiet and shy, we should kick off with a strength that might seem quite bewildering at first.

Great conversationalists!

As odd as that may sound, Introverts are in fact, great conversationalists. Not just in the sense of staying in tune with the point of discussion, they are also good listeners and what is a conversation without listening? Their outward demeanour may not seem like it, but more often than not introverts display a readiness to listen, pay apt attention and think deeply before speaking. Obviously, introverts do not eagerly initiate conversations with those who they aren't very familiar with.

However, they are very good at having and sustaining great conversations with people they connect with, like intimate friends, families and mentors. As an introvert, your distaste for small talks and public attention shouldn't put you at the rear of the crowd. Your craving for deep and meaningful conversations is valid but you never know where you might find that, so it's okay to give people a chance. It is okay to take part in small talk from time to time. Sometimes, this type of conversation can pave the way to more meaningful discussions.

Observation

Introverts are especially blessed with the ability to stay focused a lot more than people with other personalities. Why? Because introverts learn by observation. The good news is that when these traits are channelled to the business and educational field, success is never far off! As an introvert, think back to the times when you noticed things that others didn't immediately see. Your ability to focus and observe more critically is definitely a blessing, and when directed toward your career, a relationship, or even education, it can be extremely beneficial.

Creativity

Solitude is the incubator of creative ideas and nobody loves solitude like the introvert. Writing seems to be an ingrained speciality in introverts. Many introverts have second thoughts about expressing their thoughts verbally and therefore turn to writing for self-expression. Writing, however, is not the only place where introverts thrive. There are successful introverts in every field from computer programming to acting.

Prioritizing

This is one trait and strength of the introvert personality that makes them very good employees. Because of this trait, an introverted person is able to have a work and life balance. Introverts are self-motivated and can get the job done without being micromanaged. In fact, they don't like to be micromanaged.

Team Players

Surprising isn't it? Introverts crave autonomy, especially in carrying out their jobs, yet they can still be team players. For a team to work there must be unity and collaboration. While everyone is struggling to be seen and heard, the introvert isn't. Peace and unity are more important to them than being heard. This doesn't mean they have nothing to contribute to the group. Introverts are more often than not filled with ideas.

Unique Leadership Skills

While introverts are not usually deemed leadership material, they do in fact, make great leaders. Leadership is much more than a resounding voice, charming smile and a firm handshake. Introverts have the innate ability to foster deep, meaningful relationships; they are attuned to emotional cues and are able to pick up cues that might not be voiced. This is essential when there is a common goal to be achieved. Also, because they do not seek out the spotlight, they give their teammates the opportunity to shine and feel valued.

Overthinking

This might seem like a disadvantage, and sometimes it can be. But, the fact that introverts go through things countless times in their mind can also be advantageous. Why? Because, by overthinking, introverts can uncover potential problems. This can be very valuable in a work setting. As long as the introvert does not let overthinking prevent them from acting, overthinking can be a strength.

Good Listeners

This can come in handy for introverts at work, school or even in a leadership position. Listening is an important part of communication. If this trait is harnessed properly, the introvert can excel in almost every area of life.

Chapter 11: The Stigma Of Being An Introvert

Do you remember anyone from school who may have just sat or stood quietly in one corner of the room? He or she probably isolated him or herself and just observed the whole proceeding of the class. Some people will assume that person is shy—but this is a generalization that may not be true. It could be that that person is simply an introvert.

Culturally, especially in the western part of the world, the "man of action" is always favored over the "man of contemplation," so to speak. This loosely translates to a man of extroversion and a man of introversion. Why is that though? For the most part, in the corporate world, although companies try to avoid futile risks as much as possible, executives still go for the man who takes risks confidently and delivers overwhelmingly positive results. In a meeting or conference scene, the one who is more vocal about his or her ideas is the one who receives the room's attention. Extroverts, confident public speakers that they are, consistently drown out the voices of the introverts.

Introversion is usually mistaken as shyness, however, these are two separate issues. Shyness is, generally speaking, the fear of social judgment or the fear of public scrutiny. Introversion is a personality trait that describes people who prefer solitude and deep thinking, without necessarily a fear of social interaction.

The problem lies with society's view of introverts, and sometimes introverts' views of themselves. There is nothing wrong with being an introvert.

According to Adam Grant, a professor at the Wharton School of the University of Pennsylvania, introverted leaders tend to be more effective leaders than extroverts because they can manage employees well and bring wonderful ideas to the discussion.

Chapter 12: The Challenges And Benefits Of Being An Introvert

There is no question that being an introvert poses specific challenges. However, having an introverted personality can also reap huge benefits. This chapter will venture to explain both sides of this very slick coin, culminating in a list of respected and renowned individuals who used their introverted personalities to their full advantage.

Challenges

Perhaps the biggest challenge that all introverts have voiced as a common issue is avoiding hurting a friend's feelings when opting for alone time. Particularly if the friendship is a new one with an extrovert, it can be a difficult conversation to navigate. Extroverts are often less self-aware than introverts and because requiring a significant amount of solitary time is not necessary for them, they have trouble grasping the idea of someone choosing to stay home alone and read a book rather than go to a cookout. Other problems can manifest from this occurrence, such as introverts becoming overly apologetic for doing nothing wrong, feeling guilt for having potentially hurt their friend's feelings, fearing losing the friendship due to their being an introvert, and even introverts forcing themselves to become more social than they are comfortable with in order to appease a friend's feelings. While these issues do pose a host of problems, introverts can head off some of these problems by being upfront and honest with friends, which is most easily accomplished in one-on-one conversations where introverts thrive.

Similar to the issue of turning down invitations to go out are the constant comments from extroverted friends, family, and acquaintances that the introvert needs to "get out there" and increase their social activity. While these comments can usually be brushed off, maintaining relationships with friends can present a very real problem for extreme introverts, who prefer to go without social engagements for months at a time. Maintaining friendships without an overt amount of interaction has been made much easier with social media and can even be accomplished with writing letters. However, maintaining these low contact friendships is most easily accomplished when the friend is a fellow introvert. If the friend is an extrovert, one should be honest and up front with them, trusting that the friend is mature enough to understand that there are many different types of personalities that require different activities to stay energized and happy. If an introvert wishes to spend time with a friend who has invited them to a party or other large social gathering, it would be appropriate to turn down the invitation and instead offer another date to see each other in a quiet setting, perhaps over a meal or in the comfort of one or the other's home.

Some introverts have expressed that while they enjoy having alone time, the sudden craving for rich conversation with a friend can be difficult to satisfy. If the introvert has had difficulty maintaining friendships, the well of people available to get together with for dinner at the last minute can be extremely shallow. Unfortunately, this is a problem that must be solved individually as there is no easy, universal solution. In some cases, it may be best to contact a close relative or make a continual effort to maintain the friendships of at least two other people with similarly introverted mindsets.

However, when an introvert does find him or herself in the middle of a social gathering, communication can often grow difficult. Extroverts are given to quick comments, interrupting each other, and are more comfortable with shallow conversation. This is not a slight against extroverts, merely a separate set of social skills that introverts, who are skilled at intense listening and deep conversation, have difficulty taking part in. These large gatherings are not always avoidable and sometimes are required in the event of company meetings and networking. While many introverts report feeling nervous regarding these events, there are some techniques that can divert attention away from the introvert and ease some of the pressure to make small talk. In these cases, the introvert will either have to jump into the conversation or initiate a separate one with another single individual. In cases of social gatherings where the introvert does not know the majority of people, introverts should start conversations themselves with open-ended questions that will immediately place the spotlight on other individuals who may be more comfortable small talking at length.

Benefits

Although the challenges of being an introvert can at times feel crippling, there are huge benefits to this personality trait. Extroverts who tend to make a lot of plans in addition to having careers and other obligations such a family or working on health, can experience extreme stress and exhaustion from stretching their time over various priorities. However, since introverts tend to not fill up their social calendars, they have ample time for themselves, which can be used for self-reflection, recharging, or pursuing personal endeavors. The added time for self-reflection allows introverts to discover what it is that they really want from life as well as the time to reach their goals. A weekend that an extrovert may use to go out with a large group of friends and introvert can use to take a short and solitary trip to a new city and spend the requisite time exploring.

However, this is not to say that introverts dislike spending time with other people.

While all introverts experience various degrees of comfort in social gatherings, they all thrive in small groups of two to three people. When introverts choose to spend time with others, it is with people whom they have formed meaningful relationships with. Introverts dislike small talk and so their conversations tend to be far more substantial than those that occur between large groups of extroverts.

Since they are wonderful conversationalists, introverts also have piqued listening skills. Not only does this add to the quality of their friendships, it also makes introverts excellent employees. Employers can trust that introverts have taken in all of the information regarding a particular topic and made an informed decision. If the introvert works at a company that involves a high level of one-on-one contact between employees and clients, such as with sales or design, introverts are able to take what the client wants into consideration and then make discerning decisions to acquire the desired result.

Perhaps what makes introverts so successful in the workplace and in their personal relationships is their incredible self-awareness. Rarely does an introvert speak the first thing that comes to mind. Instead they will sift through their very active inner monologue and only vocalize what they determine to be the most valuable and beneficial information. This mode of thinking also helps introverts to make better decisions since they tend to be much less impulsive than their extroverted counterparts. This extends to avoiding potentially dangerous situations; when posed with the question, "if everyone jumped off a bridge, would you?" an introvert would almost always say no.

This ability to make careful decisions paired with an introvert's ample alone time makes introverts incredibly independent. While an extrovert may wait for friends to become available before going on an adventure, introverts don't need to wait and are perfectly happy to carry out plans on their own. This personality trait contributes to their workplace quality. Introverts can be relied upon to complete their work without abundant exterior help. However, introverts can also thrive in small groups, and so also make excellent members for working on a group project.

Many extroverts are under the false impression that introverts are missing out on the "fun" parts of life. However, the introvert's lifestyle is largely fueled by the independence, which in turn makes their schedules extremely flexible. It's not often that an introvert will pack their weekend with plans, which leaves them free to make impromptu trips to the museum, a restaurant they've always wanted to try, or just take some time for themselves with a walk through nature.

The misconstrued idea that there is something wrong with introverts is an unfortunate one. They have much to offer the world; a fact that is evident from the long list of introverts who have already left their mark on the world, including:

J.K. Rowling

Albert Einstein

Barack Obama

Audrey Hepburn

Bill Gates

Steven Spielberg

While these people may not immediately strike readers as introverts, they do in fact harbor many classical introvert personality traits. The eclectic group of people goes to show that while an introvert prefers to recharge in solitude rather than by being surrounded with people, they are just as capable as extroverts of excelling on a public stage.

Chapter 13: Hobbies Of Introverts

Introverts have ways of keeping themselves busy during their leisure times. Since they will not want to move out with friends or go to public places to interact with others, introverts like getting themselves involved in some activities that will include very few or no one whenever they are less busy. This is to get their energy recharged and to get themselves leisurely more engaged. Through some of those activities, introverts tend to interact with the outside world even without stepping out of their corridors. They spend most of their free time learning new things through others but without physically contacting them. However, the following are some of the things introverts do when they are not working.

Reading and Writing: While some introverts may like reading, some are good readers as well as good writers. Those who only read, read to learn more about people and things. They spend most of their free time to study the nature of things including their own nature. For instance, an introvert may spend the larger part of his leisure time reading more about himself or herself, and learning about the side of him or her that he or she needs to improve on. Those who do not read on that read about the developments that have taken place in science and technology. Some are lovers of fictional novels, and some are motivational books enthusiasts.

For the introverted writers, those write to tell the world more about themselves, that which they may struggle to do in real life. They do that through the writing of autobiographies. Those who do not write autobiographies write about some many other things to contribute their own quotas to the development of man or sometimes to show the world their talents.

Indoor Games: Some introverts are lovers of offline games while others are video games addicts. They do these to relieve themselves of the likely stresses they might have earlier passed through. Video games do not necessarily need to involve another person. One can play a video game against an online opponent or play alone without the involvement of others. Only those who play an offline game would need a direct partner or opponent. Even at that, introverts do not necessarily need many people to play with. In most cases, two players are enough to play a multi-player game. And this makes playing games one of the favorite hobbies of introverts.

Cooking: Because introverts spend most of their free time alone and often indoors, some like to eat more. Hence, those may like to cook more. Staying alone affords the introverts the opportunity to always try their hands on new types of food. To do that, they will have to go online to learn more about how to prepare such food. For instance, an introvert could spend most of his free time on YouTube all because he or she wants to learn how to prepare a delicacy.

Online Chatting: As much as introverts do not like to make so many friends, they like to make as many friends as possible online, and that always makes them active online. Although they may not be free to engage people in a face to face conversation, they always feel comfortable engaging friends online. Introverts get along really well with their online friends. Some even find their partners online since chatting with them online is a lot easier than meeting them in person. And if eventually they meet offline, they always lean on the strong bonds already formed online. Introverts like chatting a lot whenever they are less busy.

Chapter 14: Goals For Lone Wolves

There is a saying that "no man is an island" and introverts seem to live by this mantra. In everything they do, they believe they are the only ones who can do it correctly.

While it has its perks, the aloofness that comes with being an introvert incites negative impressions among friends, family and colleagues. Introverts are so enamored by their ability to work alone that they tend to shun assistance of any form. They have a sense of responsibility they think their isolation from outside forces can maintain.

At the same time, this forces people to back away from an introvert when he or she is carried away by work. In extreme cases, people tend to think lone wolves are egotistical maniacs who do not listen to advice and are so sure of themselves not to let others take the reins.

This is unavoidable. It is in the nature of introverts to have extreme levels of trust in themselves and have little or no regard for group dynamics. Needless to say, one can always see beauty of some form from this end.

Ideas are generated endlessly in a lone wolf's head. But the only problem is that he or she is unwilling to share even bits of these ideas to anyone else, for fear of being ostracized and getting unwanted attention. On the other hand, introverts are mainly theoretical creatures that feed only on abstract thinking and, in terms of application, seem reluctant to take the first step.

A lone wolf lifestyle is one that is exciting. Think about all of the quiet and unassuming personalities that built business empires out of sheer creativity. Introverts have all the powers they can get when they know it has a liberating characteristic, but it requires just as much will power to actually harness the grand abilities of a silent worker.

So, lone wolves, listen up. Here's how you can use your isolated and detached personalities to get things done.

Make time for planning

For introverts, this is similar to a walk in the park. They practically do not have any problem coming up with strategies and techniques to approach a problem. But in many cases, this is something that should be worked out, since introverts are notoriously known for being procrastinators who put off every opportunity to finish a job as soon as possible.

When you are faced with a project you know is valuable for personal and professional development, do not spare any time daydreaming about the results. Go for the shovel and start digging for important ideas to get you started. You would not waste any time as well as energy as you think things through.

Manage you time

Let me repeat what I wrote earlier: "INTROVERTS ARE NOTORIOUSLY KNOWN FOR BEING PROCRASTINATORS."

Enough said. Well, on the contrary, I did not say enough so let me just show you how important it is to manage your time. Lone wolves are, in all respects, individuals who value freedom from constraints of any form, and that includes time. Because of overconfidence, sometimes deadlines are not met. People with such an inclination towards shunning conventionality tend to deconstruct the rationale behind deadlines. Simultaneously, they often undervalue the importance of a timetable to other people (clients and professors who expect them to turn in their work, for example).

Therefore, introverts should keep their confidence in check and actually adhere to a well-organized timetable. They have all the brain power they need to provide good quality work and lead amazing lives.

But imagine them managing their time wisely to prepare for whatever may come.

Brainstorm… with other people

You mean, socializing?! GASP!

It's a real shocker but hey, when you work for an organization or you're just planning a personal project on your own, it would seem like a good idea to momentarily leave our shells and talk about what others are thinking. You would probably object to the notion of talking even if you are not up for it. But what is fascinating about introverts is that they are dedicated to a goal, to a point that they lose some semblance of their aloofness in order to collaborate and engage in discussions that also enrich themselves.

So when it comes down to actual planning, it would actually benefit you in terms of materializing whatever comes to your head. Every organization is blessed with its own ragtag team of prodigies who, if afforded the appropriate avenue for nourishment, would churn out quality work that everyone can enjoy. So in the end, wolves still need a pack for survival.

Take some time to critique

One advantage of being an introvert is you are able to see things from several perspectives. It is because of this ability to be insightful that lone wolves, in spite of their detached nature, are apparently more cognizant of defects.

What's more, being aloof means you are able to focus on the things that should improve something. You should also be able to attain a clearer grasp of the objectives you need to accomplish as a unit in a group. But it takes guts, really. Introverts tend to lose a fervor for critiquing if it means having to share one's observations with others. Still, you can get around by participating in meetings where everything is open for discussion. Criticisms are always welcome and it doesn't help if your reluctance to decide which course or project should override personal and group goals.

Apparently, we can all say that these tips for lone wolves apply only in the work place. B introverts exist in other places as well, and it is essential to know about how well you can create original plans and strategies. You have the gift of self-reliance, but it is also the same gift that makes you valuable as an employee or student or whatever.

So when you think lone wolves are cool, you are right! Because they know how to take control of their intellect and channel most of their energies towards the greater good.

Chapter 15: Friendships As An Introvert

You may have heard that if you are an introvert, you will find it difficult to make friends. This is not at all accurate. A lot of people are confused about what an introvert really is. They assume that an introvert is someone who is very shy or someone who is socially awkward and strange. The word "introverted" is thrown around a lot, but in many cases, people use this word incorrectly when they describe someone else. Being introverted means that you have a tendency to get exhausted by being around other people all the time and that you need to be alone to recharge your mental batteries. This is quite opposite to the behavior of extroverts. Extroverts are people who get recharged by being in the presence of other people. Most of us are not extreme introverts or extreme extroverts. We usually are a mix of both qualities, with one quality being more dominant. That means that we sometimes might really want to spend time alone, and sometimes we really want to be around others. Is it bad to be an introvert? Even though our society often seems to value extroverted, outgoing people more, this does not mean that extroverts end up having a lot of friends, and introverts end up having very few.

Extroverts may win in the quantity department because they tend to have many, many acquaintances, but they rarely win in the quality department as far as friendships are concerned. While extroverts may have hundreds and hundreds of acquaintances they enjoy spending time with, these acquaintances are not necessarily friendships. In fact, an extrovert may not have deep friendships with anybody. An introvert, on the other hand, prizes quality in a relationship over quantity. To an introvert, having many acquaintances will seem exhausting and pointless. An introvert prefers to collect his friends one at a time, moving slowly to be sure the relationship is worthwhile and will last a long time. Introverts are likely to derive deep pleasure and meaning from their relationships and friendships. If you are an introvert, should you try to change and become more outgoing? The answer depends on whether or not you are happy with the quality and quantity of the friendships you have. If you notice that you are feeling lonely at times because you only have one or two friends and you really would like more, then you should make the effort to become more outgoing. Take the initiative to start conversations with others more often, and accept more invitations when you receive them. If your job depends on you being more outgoing, then you will have to make the effort to appear extroverted at work, but you may find that when you are at home, you no longer wish to interact with anybody. There is nothing wrong with being an introvert. It is just a normal condition for millions and millions of people. Introverts can have wonderful, lasting, deep relationships with friends, lovers and their families. They just need to be sure they schedule some time for themselves. It is not hard to make friends if you are an introvert, you will just need to make sure you spend time by yourself when you need to be alone.

Chapter 16: How To Play To Your Strengths As An Introvert

Since the majority of the extroverted world can tend to be unaccommodating to to our introverted world, sometimes our best choice is to adapt. As always, we must do this while staying true to ourselves.

Introverts can have callings into positions of leadership just as often as extroverts. The difference is that introverts simply face different obstacles.

Even the biggest introverts are usually extroverted to a certain degree. The trouble lies within the inability to find balance.

Whether introverts want to play to their strengths in relationships or in the workplace, the same principle applies. The introvert needs to have stability and reliability.

In a busy, chaotic world, the introvert can struggle with finding a way to be heard.

Nevertheless, the introvert needs to be the decisive voice of reason.

Have you ever noticed how people tend to listen more to people who have less to say? This is particularly true if you make your words count. At one point or another, everyone has had to deal with the student in the classroom who always had their hand raised. They didn't always have the correct answer, but they always had their hands raised. Eventually, the teacher would pass them by to give someone else a chance.

Then there comes the mysterious, confident student who likes to stay quiet. When this student knows the answer to a problem, they aren't quick to broadcast it. But every time they are called on, they have a good answer. Eventually, this person becomes the go-to person when someone needs an answer.

Anyone can raise their hand and give a correct answer, but not everyone can be patient enough to wait until they are randomly called on to provide the correct answer without raising their hand.

In the same way, introverts can play to their strengths by speaking less and thinking more. Focus on making each word count. Keep it simple, yet powerful.

Modesty can speak volumes. Introverts have a tendency to let others come to them instead of actively broadcasting that they have the solution.

In the workplace, there are very few managers out there who are good listeners. There are many people in leadership positions that lack the necessary influence over their followers.

In relationships, most partners do a fine enough job at listening to each other, but few of them truly understand what the other person is going through. Asking questions about the other person isn't good enough when there is an absence of a genuine interest in the answers provided. And telling stories about ourselves mean nothing unless we enjoy telling them.

As an introvert, you have an advantage in these areas. You can be the good listener in the workplace. You can have empathy in your social interactions.

Extroverts can easily notice what's happening around them. Introverts can easily see what's not happening around them.

Since introverts have a tendency to think twice (or a hundred times) before they speak, they have an ability to work through problems that appear to have no solutions.

It comes back to the argument of quality over quantity.

One of the biggest problems introverts encounter is when we see introversion as a problem in itself. Instead of playing to our introverted strengths, we try to make ourselves extroverted.

We don't need the spotlight nor should we strive to be in it in order to be seen and heard. Successful introverts succeed not because they believe they are better than other, but because they believe they can make others better. They see their place in the world, and even though they face plenty of setbacks, they know that it's only a matter of time before they achieve true peace and joy.

Make sure you are focusing on what you can do instead of what you can get. An introverted leader might think about how they can get their followers to listen to them. This usually leads to more stress since it's based on things that they can't control. Leaders can control how well they speak, but they can't control how well people listen.

Introverts are good at minding their own business and blocking the world out. But when it comes to the lack of cooperation from others, we might suddenly make it our business. We're perfectly fine until something goes wrong. If we want to be fine regardless of what is going right or wrong, we need to focus on what we can do, not want we can get.

We need to keep creating, even if no one seems to be appreciative of our efforts. It's not about who will listen, but about how you will speak. It's not about how they react, but how you act.

Even when we feel like we're not visible, we must stay patient. If we remain solid, eventually the right crowd will come.

You can play to your strengths by embracing your uniqueness as an introvert. Embracing your uniqueness as an introvert will naturally lead to wise choices. Wise choices will prevent us from getting trapped in places that suffocate our abilities.

Whether you're at a party, a restaurant, or anything else in between, always remove the idea of commitment from your mind. One of the major reasons introverts might choose to not go into extroverted settings is the very thought that they must stay at the event for as long as it takes. They convince themselves that they must stay at parties for at least four solid hours, otherwise it would be rude to leave so early.

They might feel like failures for being unable to follow through on something they had started. But that rule does not apply in this situation. We only put more unnecessary pressure on ourselves when we choose to place these rigid sets of rules on our lifestyles.

I've noticed that the less I try to place time constraints of any sort on myself, the more likely I am to enjoy—or at least handle—the event. When I tell myself that I can leave an uncomfortable setting in an instant if I want, I usually end up staying for much longer than I had originally planned.

There are fewer bigger problems than a feeling of being trapped. Even the most horrible situation in the world is not as bad if there is the possibility of getting out.

In the workplace, we are forced to stay until the end of our shift—regardless of how horrid of a day we have had—otherwise we risk severe disciplinary action. School isn't much different.

Along the way, we have programmed these rigid and overbearing sets of limits on ourselves. We give our power away when we are unable to understand that we can live more freely.

Of course there are certain things that we need to commit to. But there are also many other things that we don't need to commit to. Don't put more pressure on yourself than you have to. Know when it's time to exit.

We need to be serious about most of the things that we do in life. But sometimes this very same seriousness is what causes even bigger problems for us down the road.

When the situation calls for you to be more extroverted, don't be afraid to mimic an extroverted person that you really respect. The good thing about this is that the person could be a fictional character. The unconscious mind doesn't know the difference. That's why you can watch a comedy movie and still laugh. If the viewer finds it funny, it doesn't matter if the film was fictional or not.

As stated earlier in this book, the fake it till you make it approach might not be enough to completely get by on. But that's why you don't fake it. The idea is to draw from the qualities that are already with you, just beneath the surface, and bring them forward. Faking it till you make it is when the quality was never really there to begin with. Mimicking a person that you really respect is matching a hidden quality within yourself to one that is significantly less hidden in them.

Summary:

- Focus on being solid instead of being heard
- Embrace your introversion

• Alleviate the pressure by remembering that there is no commitment in every situation
• Ignite the hidden quality in yourself that has been brought to life by someone that you really respect

Chapter 17: Myths About Introverts

Introverts constitute a significant percentage of some of the best thinkers and strategists in the world, but because of the many differences which they exude when compared with extroverts, they end up being misjudged and painted in a way that they aren't in the real sense. This has led to so many myths being aired around about introverts and their interesting but misconstrued mannerisms and way of life.

We have listed a few of these myths below:

Introverts are rude

They are arrogant

Hate people

Don't like to talk

I have realized that many introverted people are enclosed in their interaction with others because they feel they might not be good enough for anyone. Some feel getting close to people might deprive them of their privacy. As odd as this sounds, the truth is, a lot of kids were actually bullied into becoming introverts. They see the world as insecure and mean.

Joel (not real name) was an amiable kid. He was always the first to welcome new pupils into his class. Then one day, a new girl, Nancy (not her real name), was admitted into the class. As usual, Joel walked up to her with the brightest smile ever to welcome her, but Nancy gave him the worst embarrassment he ever had by brushing him (Joel) aside. He fell down with his face over the floor, feeling too embarrassed to get up. The whole class burst into a big laughter as Joel managed to rise in shame. The most annoying part was that Nancy didn't feel sorry about her ruthless behavior. All she said was, "I never asked for your welcome."

As for Joel, something died of him that day. He lost his sense of friendliness. Days passed, and years went away, but Joel remained the same. He would rather talk and laugh with his pen than go near anyone. He laughed alone, picked flowers alone, read novels and listened to music all by himself. He was forced into being an introvert. These are the kind of people I described as "falling within the lines." They are naturally not Introverted but were pushed into the introversion realm by situations. People like Joel could be so friendly and outspoken one minute that you begin to wonder if you ever knew them; then, the next minute they are a total non-talking stranger.

Nancy, on the other hand, might not be all that bratty. She probably had a bad day or was someone who liked been left alone- the natural introverts. Some individuals get irritated and feel very uncomfortable when others move close to them. They see uninvited friendliness as an encroachment on their private life. Nancy could be one of such. To everyone who witnessed the saga between Nancy and Joel, she was nothing but a proud brat while Joel was the one who was always putting the cart before the horse.

Introversion could be a sign of insecurity or inferiority complex. You decide to ignore the chattering of friends at a reunion party, not because you don't want to talk or do not have something to say. You do so because you see others as too good to rub minds with or too mean to understand your weakness. So, you keep to yourself and lock yourself out of the social world. The truth is, we all have our strengths and weaknesses. The people you see as gurus might jus wish they had what you have. They probably do not measure up to you.

Vital Networking tip for introverts

Networking is an essential social skill that helps to build and foster beneficial relationships amongst individuals with varying, worldviews, backgrounds, professions, and tribes. While this would always prove to be the icing on the cake for an extrovert, networking and getting to meet unfamiliar faces is always the most worrisome moment for any introvert.

To get better at this all-important skill as an introvert, a few practical and down to earth tips have been provided:

* Set a realistic goal

Before stepping out of your home or office to attend a networking event, it is crucial to understand that an event such as this isn't intended to degrade your self-worth and esteem but to provide a platform that could be beneficial to your job, career or family life.

It is, therefore, vital to set a realistic goal about the number of new persons you intend to meet, get to know and exchange contacts with at such an event. Being realistic with this would mean starting off with maybe just one new person or possibly two persons in each social event you attend.

* Understand your strength

Due to the reserved nature of introverts, they are great listeners and excellent advisors; and this is a unique ability that pulls people close to them at all times when properly harnessed. When fully armed with this understanding, networking events can turn out to be an excellent avenue to strike long-lasting alliances and to also connect with a few people at a level deeper than just the surface.

 * Start from your comfort zone

There are no hard and fast rules that dictate how to develop a social networking skill, and so if starting off at one's comfort level is the way to get it all started, then it is all great. A comfort level that works pretty well for introverts is to take out time to initiate an online conversation with one of the proposed participants for an upcoming networking event.

Doing this reduces the tension that comes from initiating a face to face conversation, and also ensures that a relationship has been established.

* Follow up on connections

One of the ways to build strong and lasting relationships from networking events is to endeavor to sustain the flames ignited during the event by keeping tabs long after the event is ended.

This means creating time for follow up calls, emails, and social media conversations, depending on the preference of both parties. This helps to blossom the established relationship, and could also imply having a buddy when at your next networking event.

Chapter 18: Overcome Your Perceived Shyness

Society today dominated by extroverts and they are seemingly more valued. This causes introverts to be anxious about themselves and struggle with their self-confidence. They tend to think that there is something wrong with their personality. However, introverts can become powerful when they embrace their quiet nature.

Accepting that you are an introvert will make you feel more confident. It will help you overcome shyness. You need to understand that shyness is a kind of fear. It is fundamentally the fear of what others may think about you. Even self-confident people find themselves in situations they are embarrassed or self-conscious, even if they don't show it.

The first thing you need to understand is that everybody doesn't have to like you and you can't please them all. It really shouldn't matter what they think, especially if they are strangers. Accepting this will be the first big step you need to take. You need to identify what is important to you, primarily, then work at making yourself happy and at ease.

To do so, you need to take stock of your values and your goals in life. Then live these values out in your quest to achieve your dreams. Throughout your journey, you will discover that there will be people who share the same values and dreams as you and there will be people who will not understand you. It's okay. Keep the right people and weed out the bad ones from your life.

Here are some practical things you can apply to help you conquer your shyness.

Whenever you're feeling shy, view the situation as an opportunity for growth.

Realize that the fear will never go away. You just get better at handling it. Try to recognize when you're feeling shy, and say to yourself, "I'm feeling shy now. If I can push through and do the thing my fear is trying to keep me from doing, next time it won't be so hard." Over time, you will realize that the most rewarding experiences tend to occur when you turn towards fear rather than running away from it. Short term pains, long term gains.

Do one new thing a week.

When you do so, you are setting yourself up for a challenge to change. As you attempt or complete one new thing every week, you are becoming more and more committed to change. You are training your mind to accept more uncomfortable things. You don't have to feel great about them in the beginning. The point is that you are acknowledging acceptance and learning new things and situations.

Guard your downtime.

Just because you are trying to overcome obstacles in social situations doesn't mean that you will push yourself to the limit. It is okay to retire from time to time to be quiet so that you will rest emotionally and mentally. When you are refreshed, you will be more ready to socialize again.

Do not forget other people when you are recharging.

Say hello to your family or friends. Be the one who makes the first move. You can use social media to check in with other people such as sending a pleasant tweet or posting a funny picture on your friend's Facebook wall.

It may take practice but remember that when you initiate the contact, you are opening yourself up and encouraging engagement.

Be prepared for group interactions.

Often, you will have ample time to prepare yourself to face a crowd, lead a meeting or speak in public. Take time and effort to organize your thoughts and feelings so you will not feel as anxious when it is time to face them.

Remind yourself that it is okay to be vulnerable.

You can start your conversation and diffuse tension by letting people know about your nervousness. It will encourage others to engage with you.

Remember, practice makes perfect.

It is okay to plan some conversation-starters. You can go for open-ended questions so people will not have to answer with simple yes or no. Asking people about themselves will also keep the conversation going.

Put yourself in sink or swim situations

You can either be shy all your life or you can go out on a limb or be on a great adventure. Take the initiative! Approach people and talk to them. Go out of your shell little by little and soon you will find it comfortable being around other people and chatting with strangers.

Going out of your comfort zone may be intimidating but if you don't take the first step, you will just stay where you are. Sometimes you need to force yourself out and enjoy the rewards of being out there.

Remember that your environment can be a stronger influence than your willpower.

Make sure to surround yourself with extroverts – friends and colleagues who are outgoing and socially confident. The more you spend time with them, the more likely they will rub off on you. It is just like practicing for and competing in any sport. You get better when you have a partner or opponent. And you improve much faster.

However, you should carefully consider that the people you choose to surround yourself. Not only should they be better than you sociably, they should also be willing to help you become better. There is no advantage to being with people who are weaker than you or who will not help you improve. Avoid people who will put you down and tell you that you suck at being sociable. Find people who love you and care about you enough to help you overcome shyness and be your very own cheerleader and coach through this struggle.

Cultivate new skills.

When you are competent, you will become more confident. Are there some things that you are passionate about? Then work to improve yourself on those things. Build your skills up. Take time and effort to acquire new learnings and experiences that will allow you to be kick-ass. Experiment on new and creative habits that will allow you to grow in your abilities and boost your self-esteem. There is nothing more empowering than feeling like an expert. As you believe in yourself and appreciate who you are, you will overcome shyness.

The most important thing in overcoming shyness is to love yourself. No matter how much you surround yourself with people who care or try out new things that build confidence, you will never see change if you don't love yourself. Learn to accept your imperfections and love yourself enough to work on yourself. This will help you act more naturally and more confidently. When you love yourself enough, what other people say won't matter. You improve yourself and overcome shyness for your own benefit, not to impress other people.

Building Up Your Confidence

It is important to know the difference between your introversion and shyness. Shyness can make you unhappy, introversion can make you powerful. Shyness can hold you back from expressing yourself. But it doesn't mean that you strive to change your personality. Being an introvert is who you are, it is part of your whole being. Shyness is an aspect that you can overcome.

The best thing that you can do, when shyness is threatening to restrain you from growing personally, relationally and professionally is to make the decision to be confident. Make it a priority. Make adjustments. When you put emphasis and importance on this goal, you will have the courage to step out of your seclusion and see a big change. Here are some things you should remember:

-   Push yourself to do things that may seem scary.

-   Set small, achievable goals and challenge yourself to complete them every day.

-   Do not despise the days of small beginnings. Remember, you can reach the mountain top by taking small steps. Nothing is insurmountable.

-   Do not force yourself to overcome shyness just because you are an introvert. When you don't have a problem associating with people or being in social situations, for example, you don't have to change. You just need to know when to draw back and recharge.

Understand that no one knows yourself better than you. So get to understand yourself more before forcing a change. Learn what motivates you. Understand your beliefs and desires deep down. It is going to be an enjoyable activity for an introvert to answer self-discovery questions because he will do it by himself. Journaling is a good way to start understanding how you tick and what ticks you off.

Most importantly, do it for yourself. You may realize that it is good to be just the way you are and there are certain aspects of your personality that doesn't have to change. Appreciate yourself even as you find out the traits and flaws that make up your personality. Are you glad that you have certain traits? Why? Are you being held back by flaws? Do not always focus on the downside of introversion, especially if it comes from others' perceptions and not from your own self-analysis. Find out what is good about being the way you are – that will boost your confidence.

For example:

-   Does introversion make you a good friend?
-   Does it make you a loyal partner?
-   Does it make you a great leader?

- Does introversion cause you to be creative?

Understand and accept that there are both negative and positive sides to any personality trait. To feel confident about yourself and avoid personality struggles, focus on the bright side.

You can become a confident, sociable introvert. Just believe in yourself, give yourself time and accept that you are a unique individual with skillsets and character traits that make a difference in other people's lives.

Chapter 19: The Introvert's Success Plan

It is easier for an introvert to conquer his fears and thrive in the social world if there is a plan that will guide him in his actions. It is also advisable to develop a plan that you can use to start developing your social persona.

Set a goal

Your first task is to set a goal for your social activities. Your goals should be related to the social activities that you have been neglecting in the past. For example, if you have not been on a date for a while, you should make it a goal to go out on dates until you accomplish whatever dating goal you've set for yourself. If you only have a few connections for business, your goal should be to meet someone new related to the industry that you are working for. You should meet someone new every week. The goal that you set depends on the areas of your social life that you have been neglecting in the past.

It is also important that your goal has certain characteristics. For starters, the goal should focus on a single area of improvement. It must also be realistic, specific, and come with a deadline. There is a huge difference between "I want to meet new people" vs. "I will say hi to three new people every week". The latter has a specific deadline and it will be very clear to you whether or not you have succeeded with your goal. If you succeed, it is important to celebrate your wins, and begin using them as momentum. If you didn't succeed, it's just as important to keep in mind that there has never been a success story without failure & lessons along the way. You should write down this quote and hang it up somewhere you can see it daily: "Success consists of going from failure to failure without loss of enthusiasm" - Winston Churchill.

Expand your social circle

The first move towards reaching your goal is to expand your social circle. If you have not gone on a date in a while, for instance, it will improve your chances to meet someone new if you spend some time with other single individuals. In the case of professional connections, you can meet new people if you begin to become active in social groups of your chosen profession. You should also identify other social gatherings where you may be able to meet other people. The easiest way to do this is to simply look up meetups occurring in your city, for your interests. Apply the lessons learned in this book thus far and push yourself to get to these events.

Spend some time with sociable people

"You are the average of the five people you spend the most amount of time with" –Jim Rohn. If your goal is to be a more sociable individual you will need help from a support system of friends. Think of those among your friend group who enjoy going out and meeting people. You want to align yourself with those people so that together you can go to social events and practice facing some of your fears.

Many introverts think that they need to be the life of the party to be able to gain social acceptance from new groups. You do not need to force yourself to become the life of the party. Going out with people who enjoy being the center of attention, will allow you to be yourself and enjoy your time in your own way. There is no weight on your shoulders to act like an extrovert. You can act naturally on the sidelines and only act towards the completion of your goal.

Explore social groups

After going to a few social events, you will be more accustomed to talking with people and improving your persona. Now that you are more confident on how you handle yourself in public, your next task is to make it a habit of going to social events. You will be invited to some of them but there are times when you need to seek out events when there are not invitations. The type of events that you seek out depends on the goals that you set earlier in the chapter.

Embrace your introvert qualities

If you still have negative thoughts about your introversion, you should change them. You should start to enjoy your alone time without guilt. In the social setting, you should be your quiet self and only add to the conversation when you feel comfortable doing so but not going so far as to filter every single thought.

Instead of acting like an extravert all the time, you should limit your use of extravert qualities to important tasks that are important towards your goals.

Chapter 20: The Challenges/Advantages We Face As Introverts In Romantic Relationships

So you have passed the tests of finding people to date and getting through the first few dates. Now you have grown and given depth to your relationship whether with another introvert or an extrovert. The next challenge as you solidify your relationship is how to keep it going and make it work.

How can you use being an introvert to your advantage in this long term committed relationship? Do you know how to use the differences between you and your partner to balance and enrich your relationship? What about the similarities – the things you have in common? How can you use these to your advantage to enrich and balance the relationship?

When you are making decisions together in this relationship, how do you use being an introvert for the benefit of the relationship? What are some of the advantages that you have as an introvert in joint decision making situations?

Indifference to the Outcome: Yes it is true that you will have a vested interest in the decisions you make as a couple. However, you will be more vested in the process than in the outcome. As an introvert, your energy and fulfillment comes from within you, so you will not be as vested in the outcome of your joint decision making as your extroverted partner may be. Yes the outcomes to your joint decision are important to you, but you will be more flexible to the outcome if you are comfortable with the process. You need less external validation than your extrovert partner does so keep that in mind.

Because you are self-reliant and self-directed, your happiness and satisfaction is again something that comes from within you. Your extrovert partner needs more external validation than you do, so if you can live with the outcome of your joint decision making discussion while letting him/her feel that their point of view prevails.

Your joint decision making will benefit greatly from the emotional depth that you as an introvert bring to the discussion. Your emotional connection with your partner allows you to offer empathy and comfort even when you disagree with his/her point of view. Your point of view might prevail, but your partner will also feel that they were heard and that their point of view was heard due to your ability to display empathy for their position. As an introvert who is grounded in your own inner world of values, ideas and beliefs, you have built a deep and

Chapter 21: Maximizing Introversion

There are a number of introverts who constantly feel that they are out of place wherever they go, especially at work, public places and sometimes in a group. It is always about who is talking more or who incites the most laugh which is a problem because talking to people and sadly connecting to most of them in a humorous level is not their strongest suit. Often, even before they become a part of a group discussion or work meeting, they have already been typecast as the "loner", quiet, shy and sometimes anti-social person. This social scarlet letter makes it even more difficult for any solitude-seeker to become a well-functioning gear in the group let alone climb the professional ladder. It is becoming clearer to them that success is tailored only to those who can gregariously command attention and forcefully implement at new idea. Brace yourself, though, because things are going to change.

As introverts are becoming more aware of the somewhat favored personalities of the extraverts, they are also realizing that their introversion is not in any way a handicap. It is in fact a very efficient tool and untapped resource that only the taciturns can access—an introverts advantage. The workforce is where every contributing member of the society spends majority of their day. There is no reason why the taciturns cannot make the best of it using their unique innate abilities to maximize its advantage.

Overcome Shyness

The taciturns do not necessarily have a fear of talking to other people outside their circle but it is not rare to find shyness in some. To some you are indeed shy, overcoming it is a task they must face first. Unlike the general public, introverts do not appreciate being thrown into the midst of people and expect for them to learn through survival. They also do not respond well to being "motivated" by force or by threats. To the taciturns, this is a form of attack and another justification why people drain their energy. The best way to tackle shyness is to allow introverts to understand the situation. Questions why and why not should be answered.

Why should you speak? Because you have ideas. In fact, they are better ideas that can help the goals of the company without taking so much risks. You are not aiming to be put on a pedestal for them, you just want to be a contributing part of the workforce and be credited for those contributions accordingly. Have you ever had a situation wherein you refused to convey your ideas and the governing body chose an idea that was so much worse than what you have come up with? Do the words "My idea was better" sound familiar? Not only was this bad idea executed, its loose conception and risk came back to make a terrible impact on everyone else's work—including yours. It is noisy chaos that can be over stimulating for an introvert. If you do not want to speak out for recognition, speak out for the sake of reducing the chaos that disrupts your concentration and solitude.

Speaking to people becomes fearful for some because conversations can lead to casual chat that can jump from one topic to another. Chats are small talks. Small talks change direction also instantaneously to just about anything. Everyone are expected to catch up and to contribute on the different subjects. Introverts are not able to go through this with ease. Not only do they need time to think about what to say, they are also very limited on the "news" or gossips in the office. Nevertheless, communication with people is the desensitizing factor in shyness.

Talk about work. Have a one-on-one conversation with a colleague at the office. The setting is very important because it lets them know that the conversation is about what you are working on and on how he can help. Talking about the job is advantageous for you because as an introvert, you would have already known what the job is all about and any questions pertaining to it you can answer with ease. It also reduces the chances of having small talks. This situation will allow you to control the flow of the conversation unlike when you are in a group meeting where the flow can come from any or every direction thus leaving you overwhelmed. It is this sense of control that you should hold on to.

Now, you may wonder by now, how to handle speaking in front of a crowd. Never fear. You just need to remember the sense of control that you learned in your one-on-one conversation. It may surprise you to know that one-on-one conversations are the hardest for an introvert. Compared to that, speaking in front of a crowd is almost a walk in the park. Why, you ask. It is the control of the flow. When you are speaking, you control the pace of the conversation. You can go slowly and no one would interrupt you or start throwing out small talks at you. As you are speaking about a subject you are an expert on, they can ask questions and you would already have the answers in your head. It is your domain and they are just bystanders. It is an introverts advantage.

Keep Doing What Works

Introverts success is dependent on how the taciturns use their innate abilities to succeed. It is not a secret that introverts learn more through observation, discern without disturbance and productive in solitude. They thrive when they are not surrounded by the constant noise in the office. When other people are satisfied with just looking the superficial aspect of the concept, the taciturns dig further and are relentless in its completion. This is an asset that employers give importance to so maximize it.

Steve Wozniak is probably the biggest supporter of working in solitude and working alone. In his little cubicle in Hewlett Packard, he created the Apple computer which is the pioneer in computer innovation. Until now, he is emphasizing that innovation is rarely achieved in a group. He has a point. Solitude is not just a state for the taciturns. It is a form of protection from the noisy world. It gives them the perfect environment conducive to how their mind works. Without the noise, nothing can disturb their thought process and they become more productive.

Work alone. Keep doing that. As an introvert, there may be countless things in your head that needs to be translated in a way that the people will understand. Disruptions and interruptions does not encourage the thought process to flow and thus must be avoided. Solitude is an enjoyable activity for a taciturn thus in the grand scheme of it all, while you work, you are also enjoying yourself. It is these little life coincidences that can make an introvert successful. This does not mean that teamwork should be abolished. Studies have shown that more influential work have been accomplished compared to what has been done by a group effort. It more of a plea to allow employees to retreat to their private spaces when they need to. Solitude can be a catalyst to excellent performance.

There is no need to advise you to only focus on one work at a time because you had probably already been doing that ever since. Keep doing it. It should not be assumed as being slow but being thorough. You divide the work in manageable sections, tackle and understand each of them and come up with solutions. Determine which of the solutions is best by examining the risks and returns. This is the perfect way to comprehend the work given to you so in any given meeting, you can stand your ground and not be left flabbergasted by questions. Any decent employer will take the quality over the number of their employee's work any day.

Learn as much as you work. This should come easy as one of an introvert's favorite pastime is reading a lot. Keep doing it. Learning constantly will always be a part of the introverts world. Not only is it a source of excitement for many but also a significant tool is success. You will never know what one information can be good for no matter how simple it is. But when the time comes, you know you're ready and fully equipped. The introverts world could possibly be the best place to train and be prepared for anything.

Exude Leadership Material

It is not impossible for an introvert to be an effective leader. In fact, the most influential and successful ones are in some ways introverted. Think Abraham Lincoln and Rosa Parks. But what can you do that can help you become one?

As an employee with seniority, other employees will look up to whether you want it or not. This is an opportunity to show your subtle but effective leadership abilities. Listen to them when they answer questions and avoid interruptions—just like how you would want it if you were talking. Listening is key to good leadership and employees respond well to those who practice it.

Remember your preference for quality conversations instead of quantity. Schedule one-on-one meetings often. These intimate arrangements will allow you to focus on a certain employees and be better acquainted with their capabilities. It is also the best way to promote trust and not make the other introverted employees left out.

Introverts leader supports the proactivity of her employees. By giving them the time to conceptualize new ideas, they function better because they set the pace of the idea themselves. Allow them to run with their ideas and respect their need for solitude when they need it. Unlike introverts, extraverts have the tendency to be threatened by their subordinates' proactivity.

You need to make use of your exceptional writing skills. Make this ability visible on your work perhaps simply through your reports and office memos. For a wider audience, create well-written pieces for the industry publication. You also have the more convenient option of using the social media to get your ideas across. The best part is that you avoid speaking and this the comfort of your home.

Recharge

It speaks for itself. Despite your efforts to be productive and an efficient leader, there will always be a time that you will crave being alone. Do not fight this urge or think of it as a liability or weakness. Solitude is the air that keeps you alive. Without it, there is very little doubt that you will become inefficient in your job.

Remember that alone time is also your source of epiphany. So make use of it.

"Did you tire yourself out thinking about it?" It was Bessie.

"Yes."

"Did that make you feel better?"

"A little bit, yes."

"If it bothers you so much, why don't you just apologize?"

"Because I'd have to talk to him again. Isn't that a bit unnecessary unless it's work?"

"Maybe. But you were a bit rude and difficult. People should always be decent enough to apologize."

Difficult. She hates that word. More than she hates the word "shy".

"Fine."

Chapter 22: Meeting Strangers

"Strangers are only strangers until you meet them. Then they are new friends."
Unknown.

Being Approachable

Before you can meet people, you need to be approachable.

If you don't signal that you are interested in someone, they won't know. For this reason, don't just wait for someone to approach you.

Begin by outwardly demonstrating that you are open and interested in meeting people.

Instead of burying your head in your phone, adopt an open body stance, put a smile on your face and look around the room.

Stand somewhere where people are sure to walk by (near the bar always works). Simply saying hello to more people makes you more approachable.

Conversation Openers

Have a simple opening line, such as "Hello, how are you?"

Compliments always work. "What a great bag you have. Where did you get it?"

Look out for similarities and highlight these. If you see someone drinking the same type of beer, there's an opener.

As you are chatting with someone or a group of people, and someone mentions they like or dislike something you feel the same about, highlight the similarity. For example, "I know! I am so addicted to that show, too!"

If you want to talk to someone, don't overthink it. Just smile, make eye contact and say hello.

Conversation Tips

A few more tips when meeting people for the first time:

Use your hands. Not only is this expressive, but showing your hands is considered more trustworthy.

When you make eye contact, gaze deeply enough into the other person's eyes to notice their eye color. Just for a moment though, as you don't want to be perceived as creepy!

Embrace your imperfections–it makes you relatable.

It's ok to use self-deprecating humor, just don't go overboard.

Asking 'why' is a great way to keep the conversation going.

Say, "That reminds me of..." as a way to steer the conversation in a new direction.

You can repeat back the last few words a person said, mirroring them, to encourage them to say more.

Avoid using slang.

Look for conversation sparks–if you see a person raise an eyebrow, that's a sign that they are interested in what you just said.

Chatting in Clusters

Depending on where you are, you may find yourself conversing in small clusters of people.

If you are joining a cluster, ask a question, or build a bridge. "How do you all know each other?" works well.

When you are introducing someone, a little gushing is ok, "This is Mary, and she is the most amazing Project Manager I have ever had!"

Tip: If you see two people in conversation, and their feet are pivoted in, this is a cue that they are engaged in a conversation that they don't want interrupted. This is a natural stance.

If you are chatting with someone, and you are open to others joining the conversation, consciously pivot your feet outwards. This will signal others that you are approachable.

Ending a Conversation

If you are having a great conversation, by all means, continue.

But if you are ready to move on, it's handy to have a strategy to wrap up a conversation.

You can do this by asking a question about future plans, such as what the person is doing later, this weekend, or on their vacation.

This creates the opportunity for you to make a graceful exit, such as, "It was great meeting you today. Best of luck during your upcoming move."

50 Conversation Starters

Sometimes all you need is a good question to get someone talking.

Browse the list below and pick out half a dozen questions that you could picture yourself asking. Next, rewrite them into your own words – and turn any closed questions into open questions.

How do you unwind from work?

What is your favorite pastime?

What are your hobbies?

What's your secret to stress relief?

What are you are you obsessed about?

Who is your favorite band? Why?

Who is your favorite singer? Why?

Who is your favorite singer-songwriter? Why?

Who is your favorite comedian? Why?

Who is your favorite actor? Why?

Who is your favorite actress? Why?

If something breaks, do you try to fix it, or do you just get a new one?

Tell me about your pets.

What's the best thing about your job?

What do you like most about your boss?

What subject did you like best in school?

Where did you go to university? What did you study?

What was your hobby as a child?

How would you describe yourself in a nutshell?

What is your favorite gadget?

What technology changed your life?

What do you still have and use that is really old?

If you were to put your name on a business, what kind of business would it be?

What would your motto for your business be?

What is your personal motto?

Where would you put yourself on the organized/disorganized scale?

What do you do to get yourself organized? How do you stay organized?

Do you still keep a paper calendar, or are you strictly online? Or a blend?

Have you ever done public speaking? What was the biggest audience? What was your topic?

Have you ever sung in public? What was your largest audience?

Have you ever done stand-up comedy? What was it like?

Who influenced your life the most?

Who did you randomly meet in your life who ended up being very important in some way?

What was the strangest coincidence in your life?

Have you experienced déjà vu?

What triggers your memories?

What is your comfort food?

Do you often run into people you know? Or not? Do you ever wonder about that?

How much sleep do you need? How much do you get?

Do you like napping? Why?

Do you ever stay up all night?

What is your favorite time of the year?

Do you like spring or fall better? Summer or winter?

What can't you live without?

What was the worst airport layover you ever experienced?

What was the best airport layover you ever had?

Where do you like to sit on a plane?

What do you always carry when traveling?

Do you experience jet lag? If not, what's your secret?

What kind of stuff gets on your nerves?

As we wrap up this chapter, here are a few helpful caveats to keep in mind:

Remember that the other people you are meeting might be a bit nervous too.

Always be ready with an open question or two.

Have a game plan going in.

What do you think? Are you feeling a bit more comfortable about meeting strangers? Can you see how these techniques will help you be more at ease when meeting new people? What are the three or four things you will do differently?

Case Studies

Rebecca found the strategies for meeting strangers helped her get over her anxiety by having a place to start. Now confident that she would have something to say and something interesting to ask, meant that she forgets about herself and just get curious about who she will meet.

Larry quickly found he was meeting more people at events simply by using the conversation starters. He was even having fun, trying out the different starters, to see which worked best for him.

Chris learned how not to be totally intimidated when meeting strangers. It was still a stretch, but the two conversation starters she memorized saved the day more than once.

Kelly had always been pretty good at meeting people but found the conversation starters gave him new ways to steer things in a different direction.

The Introvert's Survival Guide to Meeting Strangers

You are equipped with all you need to meet strangers.

Here are a few do's and don'ts to keep in mind:

Do's

DO signal that you are approachable.

DO look for similarities.

DO be generous with compliments.

Don'ts

DON'T try to talk to two people chatting if their feet are pivoted towards each other.

DON'T try to be perfect.

DON'T hide your hands.

3 Keys to Remember
KEY 1: Be approachable.
KEY 2: Build bridges.
KEY 3: Be authentic.

Chapter 23: You Do Not Owe Anybody Explanations About Your Personal Life

I know from personal experience that introverted people are more compelled to explain to others why they are doing something because they often feel that others do not understand or do not accept the way introverted act or behave. In the end, all these explanations are reduced to apologizing why we are who we are and in that way we lose a lot of our valuable energy. This was the case with me before I accepted what I am. Maybe this advice will not apply to all introverted people, but from my experience I believe that for many of them it will be supportive. Simply, although sometimes you feel it is necessary, some things you should never have to explain to other people.

1.You do not owe anybody an explanation of your life

Whether you decide to live with a roommate, alone, or out of wedlock you do not have to explain to others why you have made such a decision. Believe me, it's so liberating when you realize that you don't need to explain or to justify yourself to others.

2.You do not owe anybody an explanation for your life priorities

Want to take a break in the studies and during this period do the traveling or planning to open your own business, and put the personal life aside? Your priorities are only yours, and you don't need to justify yourself for that. Those who love you will understand and support you whatever you decide because those people know that you need those things.

3.You do not owe anybody an apology if you're not sorry

If you did something that the other person does not like, and you are not sorry about it, you should never apologize. The apology is an attempt to correct the mistakes and the impact it has had on other people. If you think you are not wrong and you are not sorry, do not ever apologize. We often apologize even though we know that we are right, and that isn't good, especially not for our self-esteem.

4.You do not owe anybody an explanation for the time you want spend alone

If you want to be alone, that does not mean that you are unfriendly or rude. You simply need to dedicate some time just for yourself. You can tell to close people in your life that you need to be alone, that's all, do not ever justify yourself to others why you need solitude. Enjoy this time dedicated only to you.

5.You do not owe anybody an explanation about your religious or political convictions and beliefs

When people share with you some of their beliefs, it's usually a sign that they have confidence in you. But just because someone shared with you his thinking, it does not mean you have to be in agreement with. Each of us has an opinion about everything in our environment, and because

we are friends does not mean we have to agree on everything.

6.You do not owe anyone to say "YES" to whatever they say

I know it's hard sometimes to refuse people, especially some that are much more demanding and pushy, but you should know your limits. If you are unable or for any reason you do not want to do something then do not. And do not worry about that, nor spend much time explaining your acts to others. Say what you have and be done with that, respect your time.

7.You do not owe anybody an explanation for your physical appearance

If you've lost weight, gained weight, grew a beard, changed hairstyle, put piercings or done something else with your physical appearance, you don't have to justify yourself to anybody.

8.Never explain why you prefer some food to the other

Everyone likes a different type of food; some prefer meat and sausages while others are more in fish and seafood. If someone is "bothered" that you will, in the restaurant where steaks are a specialty, order grilled calamari, who cares!

9.You do not owe anybody an explanation about your sex life

Whether you have an active sex life, or you're in a causal relationship, it does not need to concern anyone except yourself. People will try to condemn you because of your sexual orientation and decisions with whom you sleep, but it is not really their thing. Never let someone bothering you because you are alone or in a "socially unacceptable" relationship, it is your life and live it how you want. I'm not saying that we should not accept advice from some well-meaning person, but the only parameter is how much you are actually happy in your love affair.

10.You should never explain to anyone why you are alone

Many people find that having a partner and be in a love relationship is the only thing that is important in life. Of course, it's nice to have someone beside you, but if you are alone, it is not the end of the world. Whether you have just broken a relationship and do not want to jump immediately into another, or you may have careers now as a priority and simply do not want to get involved in some emotional stories again, it's your thing.

11.You do not owe anybody an explanation of your valid decisions regarding marriage and children

If you have agreed with your partner that you will live out of wedlock, you will not have children or maybe you do not plan marriage and children, the environment should not be given any justification. Your life, your stuff!

Conclusion

I am extremely excited to pass this information along to you, and I am so happy that you now have read and can hopefully implement these strategies going forward.

I hope this book was able to help you understand what being an introvert truly is about and how to make the most out of it and be a better, stronger person.

The next step is to get started using this information and to hopefully live a happy and fulfilling kind of life!

Please don't be someone who just reads this information and doesn't apply it, the strategies in this book will only benefit you if you use them!

If you know of anyone else that could benefit from the information presented here please inform them of this book.

Thank you and good luck!